GROWING BETTER :

LINCOLNSHIRE AND THE POTATO

Edited by Stewart Squires and Catherine Wilson

Published by

THE SOCIETY FOR LINCOLNSHIRE HISTORY AND ARCHAEOLOGY

2011

Growing Better: Lincolnshire and The Potato

First published by the Society for Lincolnshire History and Archaeology 2011

ISBN 978 0 903582 44 5

British Library Cataloguing in Publication Data
A CIP catalogue record for this book is available from the British Library

Front cover:
Everyone knows what a potato looks like but few know what the plant looks like above the ground. This photograph is of the delicate flower of the Marfona variety, seen here growing in Lincolnshire.
(GN01206, Gary Naylor)

Back cover:
Recently planted potato field near Spalding, 2004
(Catherine Wilson)

Designed by
Sue Unsworth, Heritage Trust of Lincolnshire

Printed in the United Kingdom by
FW Cupit (Printers) Limited
Horncastle, Lincolnshire

CONTENTS

ACKNOWLEDGEMENTS

A number of different authors have been involved in this book. They have written in different styles and with different approaches to the subject. The Editors have not attempted to constrain their words into a uniform style. Each chapter, therefore, stands on its own but contributes to the whole story.

The Editors wish to record their gratitude to the contributors without whose expertise the book could not have been written:

Tony Worth; Jim Godfrey OBE; Alan Stennett; Dennis Mills; Peter Dewey; Abigail Hunt; David Taylor; Charles Parker.

In addition we record our grateful thanks to the following for their enthusiasm and support for the project. Their willing involvement has greatly enhanced this history of potatoes in Lincolnshire:

David Armstrong; Ros Beevers; Caroline Benson; Bill Carter; David Chelley; Mike Cooper; Adrian Cunnington; Alan Daubney; Frank Daubney; John Daubney; Jim Epton; Fiona Fleming; Geoffrey Grantham; Rachel Green; Richard Harris OBE; Ken Hollamby; Chris Howard; Barry Jackson; Jayne Knight; Lady Elizabeth le Marchant; Gary Naylor; Graham Rowles Nicholson DL; Chris Page; Jo Parrish; Mary Powell; Ken Redmore; Sally Shaw; Peter Shepherd; Julie Squires; Graeme Stroud; John Youles.

We are grateful to the following for permission to reproduce illustrations used in this book:

Andy Weekes; Branston Ltd.; Great Eastern Railway Society; Frank Daubney; Terry Hancock; Illustrations Index, Lincolnshire County Council; Gary Naylor; Steven Hatton; Nickerson Research Centre; North Lincolnshire Museums Service; Museum of English Rural Life, University of Reading; Oldham Metropolitan Borough Council; PAS (Grantham) Ltd.; Pipers Crisps; Peter Shepherd; Tayto Group; The Potato Council; Nick Twell; Walkers Snackfoods; Adrian White; Julie White.

A particular word of thanks is due to Gary Naylor for allowing us complimentary use of a number of his splendid photographs. Others can be seen on his website at www.garynaylorphotography.com .

EDITORS' NOTE – THE USE OF IMPERIAL AND METRIC MEASURES

To ease the flow of the text for the reader the Editors have purposely avoided quoting any equivalent measure where these occur. Historically, imperial measures were always used whereas metric measures are the norm today and the text takes its usage appropriate to the period being discussed. However, to provide for any need, the following conversion factors will help.

Area	
Acre	1 acre = 4047 sq metres; 500 acres = 202.3 hectares
Hectare	1 hectare = 2.471 acres; 500 hectares = 1235.5 acres
Weight	
Pound (lb)	1 pound (lb) = 0.45 kilograms (kg)
	56 pounds (lbs) = 4 stones = 0.5 hundredweight (cwt) = 25.5 kilograms (kg)
Kilogram (kg)	1 kilogram (kg) = 2.2 pounds (lbs)
Hundredweight (cwt)	1 hundredweight (cwt) = 112 pounds (lbs) = 8 stones = 51 kilograms (kg)
Ton	1 ton = 2240 lbs = 1.016 tonnes
Tonne	1 tonne = 1000kg = 2204lbs = 0.984 tons

DEDICATION

This book is dedicated to the memory of Eleanor Bennett of Brackenborough Hall, Louth, who died on 20th October, 2009 at the age 85. The Bennett family have farmed at Brackenborough since 1908 and Eleanor was deeply interested in the farming history of the family and the area. She had been a staunch supporter of the Society for Lincolnshire History and Archaeology for many years, and gifts received at a Service of Thanksgiving contributed to the publication costs of this book.

Flower of the Marfona potato variety.
(GN01200,Gary Naylor)

FOREWORD

Tony Worth

The potato is one of the most important staple foods of the world. It provides a cheap and palatable source of carbohydrate and it can be successfully grown in most climates. Lincolnshire has been renowned for producing potatoes for generations. The fact that the County has the greatest proportion of Grade 1 land in the UK helps to make it the largest producer of potatoes in the UK. The range of soils; silts, warp land, chalk and limestone, all contribute to producing a quality potato. The Lincolnshire potato had a special reputation in the twentieth century in the London terminal markets of Kings Cross, Covent Garden, Spitalfields and Brentford, as well as markets throughout the UK. Not only were the soils and climate of Lincolnshire particularly suited for the potato's cultivation, but the entrepreneurship and marketing skills of the farmers who grew them were a major factor in their success.

This book recounts an interesting story, which deserves to be told, of the potato in the county. It tells of the families who developed the industry, the evolution in techniques, the adaptability of the crop for a range of uses and how much of the wealth of the farming industry in Lincolnshire was built on the potato. It tells of the contribution the county made in feeding the nation through two world wars, and how and why that happened. It talks of potato railways, fish and chips and potato crisps. It provides an account of the special language used by Lincolnshire people and it shows how Irish migrant labour needed at planting and harvesting was replaced by highly sophisticated machinery, early versions of which were designed and built by engineers local to Lincolnshire.

In today's world, the book tells of the research into variety, disease, storage as well as promotional activities, which is done by The Potato Council at Sutton Bridge. It tells of the transfer of knowledge not only from its own research but also from other sources both in this country and abroad. We are taken into the processes of frozen chip manufacture as well as the development of crisps and other potato based products, and how they are promoted and sold. Some through the supermarkets and some under the growers' brand names. And of course no book about the potato, whether from Lincolnshire or elsewhere, would be complete without recipes.

This is a book which anybody connected with the land or the food industry in Lincolnshire will enjoy and value. It will also be a good read for the same sort of people without Lincolnshire roots. As a member of one of the families featured in the book and as part of the process through growing, co-operative marketing to becoming a major potato packer, this book provides a very special account of where I have come from, and where my successors are going to.

Tony Worth
Patron of the Society for
Lincolnshire History and Archaeology

Holbeach Hurn
June 2011

INTRODUCTION

Jim Godfrey

Lincolnshire potatoes are renowned for quality throughout the United Kingdom; this has been achieved by fertile soils, good climate and by enthusiastic and enterprising people. In this book Stewart Squires and Catherine Wilson have brought together a number of experts to write various chapters which explain why potatoes have become such an important part of faming life, the economy and the fabric of society in Lincolnshire.

It is only 400 years ago that potatoes were brought out of South America by the Spanish and taken around the world. Potatoes are a highland tropical crop that have over several generations been adapted to the high latitude, long day length, lowland conditions and today potatoes are grown in more countries than any other food crop. They are eaten by over a billion people every day and, unlike cereals, can be harvested before crop maturity which is particularly important in drought stricken or war ravaged countries. All these attributes mean that potatoes are a very important part of global food security.

Here in Lincolnshire we are fortunate to have one of the best climates and a range of fertile soils to grow the highest yielding and best quality potatoes in the world, but as the chapters unfold in this book we can see there is more to Lincolnshire potatoes than these two physical advantages. Potatoes are one of the most challenging, interesting and rewarding crops to grow, and during the two world wars the Government encouraged food production and particularly potatoes as they produce more food per hectare than any other major food crop. The potato story in Lincolnshire is more than this, it is about entrepreneurs, the development of mechanisation, the people who worked in the fields and the development of potato products and this story is continuing today.

Alan Stennett gives a brief insight into to the history of the potato and to the growing of the crop and the part played by one of its near invisible pests, the potato cyst nematode. The Boston and Coningsby areas are noted for new or early potatoes whilst the rest of the county produces main crop for the fresh, pre-pack, crisp and chip markets throughout the UK. Stewart Squires brings to life some of the great names associated with Lincolnshire potatoes; many of their descendents are still growing potatoes today. Abigail Hunt's account of the farm workers, the women and children and the migrant, largely Irish, labourers gives an insight into their great contribution to the potato story. Their work was hard and through the passage of time without written account is largely forgotten. Many schools planned their year around the potato season allowing children to help gather the harvest.

Peter Dewey's chapter on mechanisation and Lincolnshire machinery manufacturers highlights the importance of increasing labour productivity and improving the working conditions of those working with the crop. The number of manufacturers and the list of innovations that received acclaim are impressive and no doubt led to the formation of the Lincolnshire Agricultural Machinery Manufacturers Association and its annual show that continues to this day under the acronym LAMMA. It is this mechanisation and increased productivity that allows us to have ever higher standards of living. There is also an interesting insight into the little known light railway systems used to transport potatoes from the fields before the advent of modern tractors and pneumatic tyres.

In the chapter on fish and chips, Stewart Squires vividly chronicles how the national dish developed in conjunction with the national railway system and developments in fishing.

David Taylor describes the development of potato crisps which began in Lincolnshire in the 1920s and is still an important part of potato production today. The brands established in Lincolnshire in those early days are national names today, and in the last ten years a new farmer owned brand has been established.

Then Catherine Wilson takes up the relatively recent story of frozen chips which have grown into a multi million pound business in just fifty years.

Charles Parker tells the story of the Potato Marketing Board and of the research centre and grading and packing station at Sutton Bridge. In the depressed years of the 1930s the Government established marketing schemes for various commodities and the Potato Marketing Board was born to provide adequate supplies of potatoes to consumers and reasonable prices for farmers; this helped stabilise the market and allowed investment into the potato sector so that the UK developed into the most sophisticated potato market in the world. The Sutton Bridge research facility concentrates on the post harvest and storage of the crop and has assisted British growers to provide year on year improvements to the quality of potatoes supplied to their customers for fifty-two weeks of the year. Today this unique research facility is an important component in the research and development chain in potatoes working in collaboration with other research centres in the UK and internationally. The grading and packing station was the first large scale facility of its type in the UK and pioneered the development of pre-pack potatoes which are now taken for granted by our retailers.

Catherine Wilson then brings the story up to the present day highlighting the recent trends and structure of the industry and insights from some individuals and companies currently involved in potatoes. This demonstrates that Lincolnshire continues to be the leading county in potato production and innovation, providing valuable employment and income to the county. The book concludes with some recipes demonstrating the versatility of potatoes; we must always remember that consumers are the whole raison d'être for the potato industry. Lincolnshire can rightly be proud of this buried treasure which has shaped this county and fed the nation over the last two centuries.

Chapter 1

HISTORY OF THE POTATO

Alan Stennett

Potatoes are native to the Americas – wild varieties grow everywhere from the south western USA to Chile – but the cultivated types are to be found in the high Andes Mountains of South America, where they have been cultivated for thousands of years by the indigenous populations. In their native territories, thousands of varieties are grown in an astonishing range of colours, shapes and sizes, including the purple-skinned, yellow-fleshed type preferred by the ancient Incas, but the white-fleshed potato that is best known around the world is the subspecies, *Solanum tuberosum ssp. tuberosum.* It was thought to have originated on the coast of Chile, but new genetic evidence suggests that the original location for this type is in central southern Peru.

Despite being unknown to the rest of the world until the late sixteenth century, the potato, and its American relatives, tomatoes, peppers and chillies, has made an enormous impact on the human diet, with potatoes now being the world's fourth largest food crop, grown on an estimated twenty million hectares of land.

It was brought to Europe by the Spanish conquistadores, but spread slowly at first, delayed by concerns that it might share the poisonous properties of its nightshade relatives and by scare stories that it caused leprosy as well a whole variety of other unpleasant conditions. On a more practical level, cultivation was slow to take off because it didn't fit the medieval field rotations still practised in many parts of Europe.

According to popular legend, the potato was introduced to England and Ireland by Sir Francis Drake after his circumnavigation of the world, although another suggestion is that it came to Britain by way of the North American colonies. It was again initially seen as a curiosity rather than a significant food source. In what appears to have been a characteristic British response to any new food, stories were spread that it was a dangerous aphrodisiac, although that may say more about the British attitude to sex rather than to novel foods. It probably didn't help that, according to one report, Queen Elizabeth I's chef cooked the leaves rather than the tubers, which might well have resulted in some upset stomachs since the green parts of the plants do contain poisonous alkaloids.

Potatoes did become a staple food on board Spanish ships, and it was noted that sailors who ate them rarely became ill with scurvy, a condition associated with a lack of vitamin C.

Figure 1.1 and 1.2
These two photographs of King Edward potatoes, grown on the farm of Mr Henry Harrison at Winterton, were produced to advertise the use of 'Hadfield's Guano' to increase crop yields and so supply the increasing demand for potatoes. *(Courtesy of North Lincolnshire Museums Service.)*

Scientific studies in the eighteenth century conducted by the French botanist and chemist Antoine Parmentier confirmed how valuable a food-stuff the potato was, and we now understand that it contains high levels of vitamin C and some of the B vitamins, as well as significant amounts of potassium and other minerals as well as carbohydrates and soluble fibre. Frederick the Great of Prussia is claimed to have persuaded his farmers to grow the crop by planting a large field with it, and keeping it under heavy guard. When the guard was removed one night, the local farmers, believing that this must be a very valuable commodity, went into the field, stole tubers and planted them on their own land. Peasants all over Europe soon realised how easy it was to grow and how well it yielded. They also noticed during the Napoleonic Wars that marauding armies were less likely to steal potatoes from the fields than they were to take harvested grain. Production therefore rose dramatically, especially in Ireland, where the wet conditions made other crops less reliable; and Northern and Eastern Europe, where it thrived in colder conditions. It also provided the fermentable raw material from which poteen, aquavit or vodka could be distilled, thereby allowing the locals to thrive in colder conditions.

The reliance on the crop caused a disaster in Ireland, where the *Lumper* potato variety proved to be particularly susceptible to a new disease, potato blight, which could reduce a field of tubers to a rotten mush in a few days. Blight spread rapidly, helped by the limited genetic variation in the crops, and contributed to the Great Irish Famine of 1845-49, in which it is estimated that up to a million people died, while a similar number left the country to emigrate to America or the Antipodes.

In England, the potato is credited with being one of the driving forces behind the industrial revolution, since workers, even in towns, could still grow a significant part of their daily requirements on a small garden plot, and the introduction of the railways meant that potatoes could be moved quickly and easily from areas where they could be grown in large quantities *(Figures 1.1 and 1.2)*. *(See Chapter 6)*.

Lincolnshire was one of those areas best suited to growing the crop. The silt and peat soils to be found in the Fens and on the Isle of Axholme are excellent growing mediums for almost any crop, but potatoes thrived there particularly well. The crop was almost certainly well established in many parts of the county by the late 1700s, and by the early part of the next century an 'export' trade had already developed from those parts where river or canal communication allowed for easy transport of this bulky commodity. The railways accelerated the trend towards specialist growers on the better soils. On the Isle of Axholme, served from 1849 by the Manchester, Sheffield and Lincolnshire Railway, the crop was popular on 'warp' lands. These were where river water with a high silt content was allowed to flood the fields in the spring so that the fertile material settled out onto the land. Large amounts of manure were also brought into the area from the industrial cities to increase the yields.

Further south, a number of specialised growers set up in business in the Fens, where the Great Northern and Midland and Great Northern Railways offered services to London and the industrial cities of the Midlands and the North. The most notable example was William Dennis, from Kirton, a farm labourer who built up a farming business covering over 4,000 acres at the start of the twentieth century *(See Chapter 3)*. About a third of his land was down to potatoes at any one time, and he is reported to have sent two thousand wagon-loads of potatoes from Kirton station alone in 1904.

The same period saw a huge interest in breeding new varieties, with amateur and professional breeders looking for new types that yielded well and resisted blight. Lincolnshire seedsmen and growers were at the forefront of the search for better options, and the business became as competitive as the great Dutch tulip fever. One report from 1904 claimed that six pounds of *Discovery* seed potatoes – costing 3/6 per tuber – had yielded a crop worth over £530, and had not succumbed to blight despite it being 'a record wet year' in south Lincolnshire. The following year, a Mr Scarlett, from Spalding, is reported to have paid twenty-five pounds for a single tuber, and then sold one eye out of it for five pounds! *(See Chapter 3.2)*. William Dennis made his start with a variety called *Magnum Bonum*, and the most basic of Latin scholars can work out that it was making big claims, while John Butler, from Scotter, *(see Chapter 3)*, took a variety that had been discarded by a Yorkshire grower, renamed it the *King Edward*, and

Figure 1.3
Potatoes growing at Stenigot, high on the top of the Lincolnshire Wolds in 2011.
The stony nature of the soil is very evident. *(Stewart Squires)*

established a variety that is still grown and appreciated today. Charles Sharpe of Sleaford, *(see Chapter 3)*, offered dozens of new types in his catalogue, including *Sharpe's Express*, introduced in 1901 and still available as a heritage variety from specialist growers, or as seed potatoes for gardens or allotments.

Potatoes have remained one of the core crops of Lincolnshire farming, thanks to the innovations in techniques and equipment introduced by people like A.H. Worth *(see Chapter 3)*. He was one of several farmers who laid down complete railway systems on their land between the wars to allow the crop to be harvested under conditions where a horse and cart, or even one of the early tractors, could not move on the wet land in autumn and winter. Ralph Godfrey *(see Chapter 3)* took the crop up onto the Lincolnshire uplands, away from its traditional fen, warp and carr soils, while Clifford Nicholson *(see Chapter 3)* by growing *King Edwards* on the higher limestone grounds, made it a premium crop *(Figure 1.3)*.

The pre-eminence of Lincolnshire as a potato county was confirmed in 1941, when Sir John Russel wrote that 'potato growing in Lincolnshire has now become a great art'. He praised local farmers for their cultivation methods and choice of varieties, but added that, in a poor season, they would 'lose money by the hatful'. Some things never change.[1]

Endnote

1 John Russel, *English Farming*, William Collins, (1941).

1.1 LINCOLNSHIRE DIALECT

Stewart Squires

Figure 1.1.1
'Tates' advertised for sale at a farm gate near Hainton, between Louth and Wragby.
(Catherine Wilson)

Growing up in Lincolnshire in the 1950s and early sixties I always knew what potatoes were. They were growing in the fields around the village and there were opportunities for some cash to be earned by potato picking. They were also always to be found growing in both my father's and grandfather's gardens and there was great excitement in digging them up fresh for the day's meal. So, I knew what they were but I rarely heard them called potatoes.

Looking back with the benefit of hindsight I was then living in an age of transition as far as dialect was concerned. I heard the terms used by my grandparents from the late Victorian period when everyone used the local dialect. So they talked about *Taaets* and *Teeuts* and, picking up on that and modifying it for our use as youngsters, we called them *Tates*, *Taters, Tatos* or *Taties.* We also called them *Spuds*, although this we were aware was a term understood nationally. A spud as we knew it was a narrow bladed spade used for digging root vegetables from the garden, including lifting a few potato tubers to supply the daily meal.

Pot's is something we never called them but which was, and still sometimes is, a spelling used by greengrocers and market traders, much to the annoyance of those educated to understand the use and misuse of the apostrophe.

So, we did not talk about potatoes as a vegetable. We did have potatoes but they were holes in your socks where the toe bulging through looked just like a new, albeit very small *Tatie.*

These words are still in use today and signs at farm gates can still be seen advertising *Tates* for sale. If you come across one please stop and buy some and help to keep some Lincolnshire dialect going.

Chapter 2

POTATO CULTIVATION

Alan Stennett

The potato is an accommodating crop, which can be grown under a wide range of soils and climatic conditions, but to grow and yield well it prefers a fertile, well-cultivated soil and a mild climate with adequate, but not excessive rainfall. Lincolnshire, with its high quality soils, cool temperatures and regular, but relatively low rainfall suits the crop very well.

The plant

The potato plant is an herbaceous perennial which fruits and sets seeds as well as growing the familiar tubers on its roots *(Figure 2.1)*. New plants can be grown from the seed, often known as true seed. This system of propagation is used to help develop new varieties, but for commercial use the crop is grown from the tubers. Cultivated in this way, it is capable of giving substantial yields. The world record yield from a single plant stands at 168 kg, and commercial crops of up to 100 tonnes per hectare have been grown, although a more typical UK yield would be forty to fifty tonnes per hectare. It is also a very adaptable one, as can be seen from its wide distribution in its native habitat – anything that can grow anywhere from Alaska to the coast of central south America by way of the high Andes has to be able to deal with a wide variety of conditions, but the better the conditions, the better the crop.

Figure 2.1
Cara Potatoes in flower.
(GN 01204, Gary Naylor)

Types and varieties

About eighty varieties of potato are grown in the UK, usually divided into first and second earlies and maincrop, although there is considerable overlap in their seasons and uses. Main crop types are themselves also subdivided into early or late main crop, and in categories depending on their intended use, with some preferred for sale as fresh produce, or for chipping, while others go into processing sectors such as crisp or starch production.

Traditionally, first earlies, also known as new potatoes, were grown in favoured locations such as Jersey, Cornwall or Pembrokeshire, but the use of fleece or clear plastic to warm the soil has allowed production to spread to many other parts of the country. In Lincolnshire varieties such as *Premiere* and *Rocket* are most often grown on the very light sand soils near Coningsby. Yields are low for first earlies, with growers relying on the premium price associated with the product.

Second earlies are left in the ground for longer, to allow the crop to bulk up to a heavier weight, and to allow the skins to set, making transport and storage easier.

Figure 2.2
Crop mechanically defoliated for salad potatoes.
(GN0978, Gary Naylor)

Just to add to any confusion over naming, types such as *Estima*, *Marfona* and *Nadine* are often the 'new' potatoes advertised by fish and chip shops as they switch over in the early summer from stored old crop to newly lifted tubers. The very small tubers, often described as Boston new potatoes, having been grown on the excellent soils in that part of the county are often second earlies such as *Maris Bard* that have been lifted well before they reach maturity *(Figure 2.2)*.

Main crop comprises about 80% of all the potatoes grown in the UK, and includes such varieties as *King Edward, Cara* and *Maris Piper*. The crops are lifted later in the year, with large amounts held in store to supply the market over the winter.

Rotations

To reduce pest and disease levels, potato crops should not be grown too frequently on the same land. Many fields that were used too often for the crop during and after the Second World War built up such high levels of soil nematodes that they remained unsuitable for the crop for many years afterwards, in some cases right up to the present day.

Soils and climate

The potato can be grown on almost any type of soil, except saline and alkaline soils, with a pH range of 5.2-6.4 being preferred. Naturally loose soils, which allow the tubers to grow more easily, are preferred, and loams or sandy loams containing high levels of organic matter, with good drainage and aeration, are the best options, although Lincolnshire growers have successfully produced the crop on everything from heavy clays to the limestone brash of the Wolds. Light soils offer the benefit of easier cultivation, but with the drawback of not holding moisture well and therefore needing irrigation. Heavy soils cause problems at lifting, particularly in wet seasons, although they do hold water well and allow the crop to continue to grow even in dry spells.

The optimum temperature for the varieties grown for commercial production is around 20° C, and growth is inhibited below 10°C and above 30°C. Rainfall needs to be enough to maintain good soil moisture content without creating high humidity conditions that encourage diseases. Most temperate zone crops require a rainfall level of 500-650 centimetres per year, with the greater proportion required in the later tuber-filling growth stages. Where the supply is inadequate, or the soil particularly well draining, the supply can be supplemented by irrigation.

Preparation

A good seed bed is a vital requirement for potato production. The crop is planted in the early part of the year, on land that will normally have been ploughed in the autumn or early winter after the previous crop was harvested. Frosts and other weathering during the winter will help break down the sod, which can then be

Figure 2.3
A potato showing new shoots (chits),
now ready for planting.
(GN02060, Gary Naylor)

harrowed or cultivated into the final bed, which should be soft, well-drained and sufficiently aerated. The process will also clear the crop of weeds, volunteers from previous crops and some of the roots remaining from the previous year. Organic manures should also have been incorporated during the cultivation process.

Potatoes are a 'greedy' crop, so inorganic manures, principally nitrogen, phosphorous and potassium (N, P and K) are added to the soil shortly before or during the planting process, although some N may be applied to the crop during the growing season. Other nutrients, such as magnesium may also be incorporated if soil tests reveal a need for those inputs. Amounts and proportions of the various nutrients will vary according to the type of soil, variety being grown and the intended use of the harvested crop.

On soils with a high proportion of stone or clods, mechanical de-stoning may be used to reduce the risk of unwanted lumps being carried through the harvesting process and of damage to the crop by bruising during lifting and cleaning.

Seed potatoes usually need to be chitted – allowed to form the first new sprouts – before being planted *(Figure 2.3)*. This has the effect of accelerating the whole growth cycle, since, once put into the ground, the new plants can be expected to emerge more quickly and to start tuber initiation faster. This offers the option of a longer growing period and therefore greater yield or the ability to harvest earlier to catch a better market or to allow lifting before the worst of the winter weather. This practice is almost universal for early crops, and is still popular with many Lincolnshire growers for main crop varieties.

Planting

As mentioned earlier, the potato crop is usually grown not from true seed but from 'seed potatoes' - small tubers between thirty-five and fifty-five millimetres in size. It is important that such potatoes are healthy, free of pests and of a single pure variety. Most seed planted in the UK is grown in Scotland, in areas where great care is taken to ensure the necessary high quality *(Figure 2.4)*. A major advantage of the area is that the aphids which spread many potato diseases are not present this

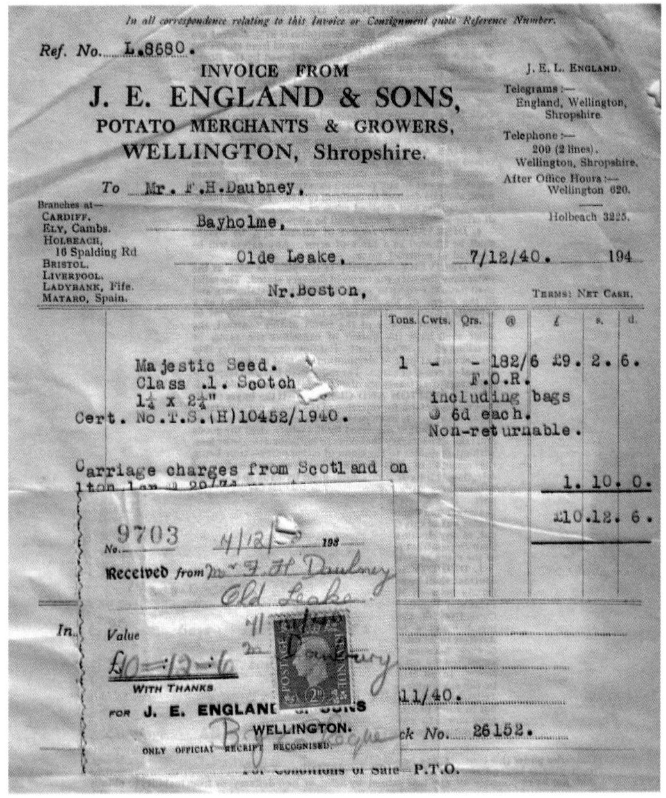

In all correspondence relating to this Invoice or Consignment quote Reference Number.

Ref. No. L.8680.

INVOICE FROM
J. E. ENGLAND & SONS,
POTATO MERCHANTS & GROWERS,
WELLINGTON, Shropshire.

J. E. L. England.
Telegrams:— England, Wellington, Shropshire.
Telephone:— 209 (2 lines). Wellington, Shropshire.
After Office Hours:— Wellington 620.
Holbeach 3225.

Branches at— Cardiff. Ely, Cambs. Holbeach, 16 Spalding Rd. Bristol. Liverpool. Ladybank, Fife. Mataro, Spain.

To Mr. F.H.Daubney,
Bayholme,
Olde Leake,
Nr.Boston,

7/12/40. 194

Terms: Net Cash.

	Tons.	Cwts.	Qrs.	@	£	s.	d.
Majestic Seed. Class .1. Scotch $1\frac{1}{4}$ x $2\frac{1}{4}$" Cert. No.T.S.(H)10452/1940.	1	-	-	182/6 F.O.R. including bags @ 6d each. Non-returnable.	£9.	2.	6.
Carriage charges from Scotland on 1 ton ...					1.	10.	0.
					£10.	12.	6.

No. 9703 4/12/40 193
Received from Mr F.H. Daubney Old Leake
Value £10=12=6
With Thanks
for J. E. England & Sons
Wellington.
Only official receipt recognised.

...11/40.
...ck No. 26152.
... Conditions of Sale P.T.O.

Figure 2.4
An invoice, dated December 1940, for the sale of Majestic seed potatoes, delivered from Scotland to Old Leake. *(Courtesy of F. Daubney)*

far north. Seed of some varieties is imported into the UK, mainly from the Netherlands. It is possible for farmers to grow the crop from seed saved from the previous year's production, but the reduction in cost has to be weighed against the higher risk of pest or disease contamination.

The tubers are planted in a furrow which is then closed over them – earthing, hilling or ridging up - to create the familiar ridge and furrow appearance of the potato field. De-stoning is often carried out at this stage, with the stones and clods left in the bottom of the furrow between the plants. Planting can also take place in two or three row beds, each the width of two rows, with furrows at an appropriate distance for the wheel spacing of tractors and other implements.

A soil temperature of about 7°C is recommended for planting, which is usually ascertained by a more reliable system than the reputed old test of applying a bare bottom to the soil to find out whether it is warm enough!

Figure 2.5
Potatoes growing in their ridges. (GN04533, Gary Naylor)

Ridging up

The ridges in which the crop is growing need to be kept intact to ensure that the plants remain protected, and to ensure that any tubers that form close to the surface are well covered. Tubers exposed to the light turn green as a substance called solanine is formed. Although solanine and similar chemicals do contribute to the flavour of the crop, they are toxic in higher concentrations and their presence reduces the value of the crop to the grower. Ridging up also increases the yield of the crop and affords some protection against blight *(Figure 2.5)*.

Weed control

Once the potato crop has become established, the large area of foliage is a good weed suppressor, but controlling weeds in the early stages of growth is important to reduce competition for light and nutrients. A pre-emergence herbicide is often used to control weeds that come up before the crop emerges. The treatment may also include a contact herbicide to kill off any weeds that have already germinated. Once the crop has emerged, herbicides chosen to avoid crop damage may be applied. Mechanical methods such as hoeing or harrowing are also effective at this stage, and their use may be combined with re-ridging the crop to ensure that developing tubers are not exposed to the light.

Pest control

The most significant insect pest affecting potato crops worldwide is the Colorado Beetle, which can rapidly defoliate a crop, but, fortunately, it has not yet become established in the UK. Other 'overground' pests include the turnip moth and the click beetle, whose larvae can damage the tubers, as well as the aphids which carry a number of viruses that affect the crop. Control of all is achieved by the timely use of insecticides to kill the pests themselves or their larvae.

Soil-dwelling Potato Cyst Nematodes (PCNs), also known as eelworms, are the most widely distributed pests of potatoes in the UK, affecting both yield and quality. It is estimated that they cause up to a ten percent loss of potential yield every year. Cysts containing the eggs of the pest remain in the soil until a new crop is grown, at which point chemicals released from its roots stimulate the cysts to hatch out a new generation of the pests. These then attacks the roots of the growing crop, damaging its ability to grow and permitting the next cycle of cysts to form. These can then remain dormant in the soil for many years, until potatoes are grown once again in that field. A 2008 study carried out for the British Potato Council concluded that to control PCNs by rotation alone would require a period of at least twelve years between crops, but that figure can be reduced to one year in five or six by the use of nematicides or 'trap' crops which encourage nematode egg to hatch but prevent the pest from multiplying. Resistant cultivars to one of the two main types of PCN can be grown, which also have the benefit of encouraging egg hatch without permitting multiplication. Partially resistant varieties to the other type are becoming available, but are still liable to losses from root damage by the pests.

Figure 2.6
Applying nematicide and planting potatoes in one operation. (GN03477, Gary Naylor)

Slugs are a constant problem to potato growers, since they attack the growing tubers, reducing the quality of the crop and allowing disease organisms to gain access to the body of the potatoes. Control is usually by means of pellets containing nematicides scattered onto the ground round the plants *(Figure 2.6)* but their use has been coming under scrutiny because of residues being detected in water courses. An alternative is the use of a biological control consisting of parasitic nematodes which are sprayed onto the soil and which attack the slugs themselves.

Disease control

Potatoes are prone to a number of bacterial and fungal diseases, most of which are difficult to control by chemical means, since they attack the new tubers under the ground and are therefore not accessible by spraying. Fungicidal seed treatments are available, but the majority of control measures are cultural. Choice of variety, quality of the seed stock, good seed beds, regulation of soil moisture levels and acidity, and controlling the insect vectors of some diseases all play a part.

The principal exception, and the potato grower's biggest problem, is late blight, *phytophthora infestans*, a fungal disease which caused the Irish potato famines of the nineteenth century. The disease first attacks the haulm – leaves and stems - of infected plants, causing them to rot and die. Spores from this first stage can then drop onto the soil to infect the tubers, which also rot away.

The disease is often spread from material such as dumps of potatoes not fit for sale, haulm left out in the fields, old potato clamps and volunteer plants carried over from previous years' crops. Removing such sources of infection lowers the risk, but spores can still drift into the crop from locations further away, often during a so-called 'Smith period', a combination of warmth and high humidity. Organisations such as the Potato Council maintain an early warning system to alert growers to Smith periods, which allows growers to initiate a programme of protective fungicide sprays to prevent the disease from getting established. Regular spraying normally offers good control, although there have been reports that the disease is resistant to some products. The risk is greatest during wet conditions which, unfortunately, are also likely to hinder the use of sprayers or other machinery.

The arrival in Europe of a second type of the fungus has increased the possibility of increased resistance to fungicides since the two strains can now reproduce sexually to deliver a greater genetic variety to the new generations. This provides new opportunities for the disease to develop resistance to the chemicals used to control it.

Irrigation

Irrigation can offer significant yield benefits on lighter soils and/or in dry weather conditions, since the relatively shallow roots of the crop make it vulnerable to water stress. The technique also offers the ability to target a higher quality market with a more uniform, better finished product. Rain guns and movable booms are still the main methods of water application, but the rising cost of water and tighter limits on the amounts that can be used have seen an increase in the use of trickle irrigation, where pipes laid in the field apply a measured small amount to each plant as required. Irrigation is most valuable in the middle to later part of the growing season, since that is the stage at which the tubers are forming and filling, a process that requires more water *(Figure 2.7)*.

Irrigation should cease before the crop is harvested. The crop will then use up what water is in the soil, leaving it in a better condition for lifting than if the soil is wet. Since irrigation water has to be paid for, it also reduces the cost of growing the crop.

Burning off

To make lifting the crop easier, especially when it is necessary to lift before the foliage has died back, growers burn off the haulm. This may be as a way of controlling the size of the tubers as growth stops when the haulm is removed or dead; getting a better skin set so that the crop can be stored more safely; removing the green material that would otherwise tangle up the harvesting machinery; or reducing the risk of the spread of disease or tuber blight – sometimes a mix of several or all of those reasons. To eliminate the blight risk and to ensure a complete die-back of the foliage, two weeks are normally allowed between burning off and harvesting.

The usual method used to be to spray the crop with sulphuric acid, but this has attracted criticism on environmental grounds and the possible risk to the health of workers using acid, and it has been banned as from 2010. Other products such as diquat, glufosinate and carfentarzone have now largely taken its place *(Figure 2.8)*.

Physical methods of haulm destruction, such as flailing or root cutting are also important, and in some cases a combination of the two, for example flailing to reduce the height of the haulm followed by a desiccant to burn it off, can be economic and effective.

Figure 2.7
Irrigating the crop using a Briggs boom. (GN04564, Gary Naylor)

Lifting
After the appropriate period of burning off, or when the crop has fully matured – indicated by a yellowing of the leaves and the easy separation of the tubers from the roots - the crop is ready for lifting. The job is done by a harvester that opens up the ridge and lifts the tubers, any remnants of haulm, and the surrounding soil onto a moving chain bed that allows soil to fall back through onto the ground. Haulm, clods and stones are also removed at this stage, and the crop is transferred to a trailer or into boxes to be moved off the field. Care in handling and moving the crop is essential at this stage, since any bruising caused by knocking against parts of the machine or stones can leave the tubers open to infection while in store. Avoiding long drops while being moved from one part of the machine, or into the trailer or potato boxes, is a vital part of this protection. Some crops destined for immediate sale may also be bagged in the field ready for moving to wholesale markets or direct to customers.

Storage
The newly harvested tubers are living tissue, so when they have been lifted they continue to respire, producing heat and carbon dioxide, and to lose water. Proper storage is essential to prevent post-harvest losses. The days of the old potato 'pie', where the tubers were heaped into a long row and covered with straw and earth are long gone, with storage now mostly in ambient or controlled condition stores.*(See Chapter 10.1)* In either case light is excluded from the store to prevent greening, with its risk of toxic products being formed in the tubers. Ventilation is used to dry any surface moisture from the crop, and a period of conditioning helps to firm the skins and assist the healing of any wounds or damage inflicted during harvesting.

Figure 2.8
Haulm following burning off using chemicals. (GN 0979, Gary Naylor)

Once this conditioning, or curing, is complete, the store temperature is reduced to slow respiration, prevent sprouting and to help stop rots and tuber blemish diseases developing in the store. Sprout suppressant chemicals may also be used to help maintain the crop in good condition, although pressure from retailers and other users means that alternative methods are usually to be preferred. Ethylene gas has also been used as a suppressant, which leaves no residues on the tubers.

Ambient stores, which do not involve refrigeration, are generally only used for shorter term storage, but conditioned stores, using cooled air with controlled humidity and carbon dioxide levels can maintain a crop in good conditions for up to a year.

Storage conditions will vary according to the intended use of the potatoes – potatoes for fresh consumption can be held at 1-3°C for long periods, but those intended for processing should be held between 7° and 11°C since too low a temperature encourages the conversion of the starch in the tubers to sugars, which make the finished products too brown.

Research on potato storage methods is carried out in Lincolnshire at the Sutton Bridge Experimental Unit of the Potato Council. *(See Chapter 10.)*

2.1 Growing the Traditional Way

Catherine Wilson

Growing potatoes today is a highly sophisticated and scientific process. Precise chemical treatments can be applied and adjusted depending on the needs of individual fields, varieties being grown, end use, and weather conditions, both to fertilise and prevent disease. Both planting and harvesting are completely mechanised, using people only to drive the machinery. But it is only in recent years that this has been so. A gradual process of increasing mechanisation has taken place since the Second World War but older people can still remember a different way of doing things.

Figure 2.1.1
Brook's Farm, Leverton, c.1950,
showing glass chitting house at bottom right.
(Courtesy of the White family, Old Leake)

For a large part the twentieth century growing potatoes was a labour intensive and back-breaking job carried out by man and horse power. Over the winter, the soil was prepared in the usual way. At the start of the season, seed potatoes would be laid in wooden trays and placed in a light airy place, often a large glass house, to encourage the production of the first shoots (chitting) *(Figure 2.1.1)*. After planting, the wooden crates were carefully stored and kept for next year. If possible they would be stored undercover but some farmers would go to great lengths to keep them dry. *(Figure 2.1.2)*

Then the trays of chitted potatoes were taken to the field where a 'ridging' plough was used to create a deep furrow into which the potatoes were set by hand at regular intervals. In the days of horse-drawn equipment this would be done one furrow at a time; progressing sometimes to a three-row ridger behind a tractor. Some of these were equipped with seats on which the operatives sat to drop individual potatoes into the furrows. This was perhaps slightly less uncomfortable than walking behind the plough and bending right over to place the potato in the furrow, but still fairly hard on the back.

Figure 2.1.2
Brook's Farm, Leverton, c.1950,
showing a thatched stack of chitting trays.
(Courtesy of the White family, Old Leake)

The control of weed growth after planting was important to prevent the new potato shoots being choked. Before the common use of herbicides to kill them, the weeds had to be physically removed by hand or horse drawn hoe. The number of people engaged in this task, illustrated in *Figure 2.1.3,* gives an indication of how labour-intensive this

Figure 2.1.3
Line of men employed as a gang to hoe potatoes on a Sunday, due to labour shortage, 1917.
(MLL8990 from the Illustrations Index by courtesy of Lincolnshire County Council)

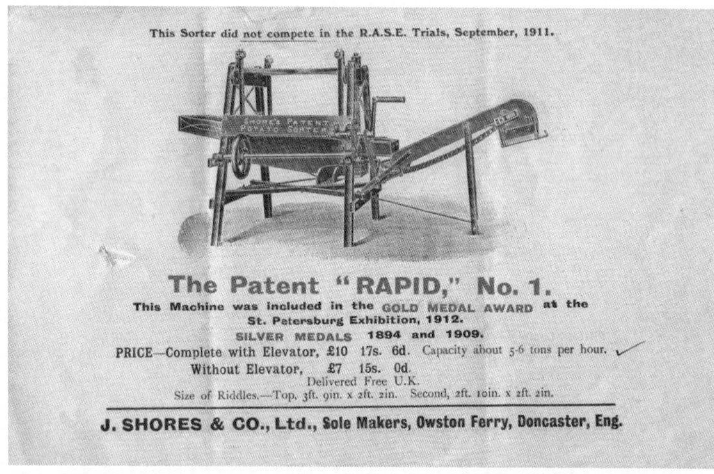

Figure 2.1.4
The Patent 'Rapid' No. 1 potato sorter made by the small company of J. Shores & Co. Ltd. of Owston Ferry. *(Charles Parker collection)*

process was and yet it had to be done to ensure the potato plants would grow on strongly.

The pests and diseases which affected the potato crop were much less well understood than they are today, and fewer chemical treatments were available so getting a good yield was less predictable.

When it came to harvesting, the potatoes were lifted by means of a special plough or spinner which brought them to the surface but then they had to be gathered by hand. This potato picking was all piece work. The potato rows were divided into *reches* (reaches). Each person in the gang of pickers would be allocated a 'rech', or perhaps a *rech* would be shared if children were doing the picking. The gang for that day, whether they were family or hired labour, would be allocated a *rech* at a time and spread out down the row to pick the crop by hand into woven willow baskets with a hand hold on each side known as *mollys*. This could be a cold and dirty job and the constant bending made it very hard work. When a basket was full it was tipped into a horse or tractor drawn cart standing nearby and the basket taken to be filled again. At the end of the day the workers were paid according to how many *reches* they had picked.

Once harvested, the potatoes were not cleaned or treated in any way but, by hand, were put straight into clamps, or into sacks if they were to be sold straight away. They would stay in the clamps until required, which could be in the depths of winter, when a clamp would be opened and special potato forks, with bulbous ends to the tines to prevent damage, were used to lift the potatoes into hand held riddles which would separate out undersized potatoes and allow rotten or green ones to be picked out by hand. A sophistication was a riddle stand on which to rest the riddle; then hand-operated wooden sorters were introduced *(Figure 2.1.4)* but real 'luxury' was a motor-driven potato sorter which speeded up the work considerably. After sorting the *ware* was put into sacks for transport to the point of sale. All this was outdoor work and the cold and discomfort can be imagined. *(See also Figure 10.2)*

Chapter 3

THE PEERS OF THE POTATO

Stewart Squires

There were a number of men in Lincolnshire who were involved with the development of the potato industry, discovering new varieties and supplying seed. Some have names that are familiar today, others less so. Some farmed on a very large scale and were the founders of what we now know as agribusiness. Today's large landowners are sometimes called 'Barley Barons'. Some of the men in this chapter could be better called 'The Peers of the Potato'. Three in particular, George Caudwell, William Dennis and Arthur Hovenden Worth, deserve this recognition as the pioneers of the industry. Others were involved in the production of seed potatoes and the growing of potatoes successfully on a variety of soils. The list does not intend to downplay the role of others but is presented as an example of the entrepreneurial skills that have led to the Lincolnshire potato industry being what it is today. Some examples of growers and suppliers today will be found in *Chapter 11*.

John Butler

John Butler was a grocer and draper in Scotter, between Gainsborough and Scunthorpe. In the mid 1890s he started farming and his letter heading in 1903 stated he was a 'celery, carrot and seed potato grower', with four farms at Scotter, Scotton and Messingham. In 1904 he had nine farms.[1]

A potato variety called *Fellside* had been bred in Northumberland in the 1890s and passed on to a grower at Snaith in Yorkshire. Butler's claim to fame is that he bought up all the stocks of this variety and rebranded it to become one of the best known varieties to this day. It was first marketed in 1902, the year of the Coronation of King Edward VII, hence the *King Edward.*

George Caudwell

George Caudwell was a farmer living at St Lambert's Hall at Weston, to the north east of Spalding. By the 1930s he was farming an estate of some 3000 acres, half of it producing potatoes.[2] Like many other farmers on the fens by the early twentieth century he was growing increasingly large acreages of potatoes. He was also experiencing problems with handling the quantities of both seed potatoes to plant and the transport of the potatoes he lifted from his fields to and from the places where he could link up with the existing transport systems. A great innovator, it is to him that the credit must go for that revolution in farm transport, the light or 'potato' railway, laid within the fields.[3]

Most work related to growing potatoes requires access to the land in the autumn and winter months, the very months when access was most difficult due to the wet ground conditions. Caudwell thought that a railway might solve his problem and contacted the well known Lincolnshire machinery supplier, Peacock and Binnington, for a quotation for one mile of standard gauge railway. Following discussions with Henry Peacock, a German firm with extensive experience of providing narrow gauge railways in West Indian sugar plantations was asked to survey the chosen site, Wraggmarsh House Farm, purchased by George Caudwell in 1908, and a narrow gauge railway was proposed. Unconvinced, or simply an astute businessman, Caudwell was persuaded

Figure 3.1
George Caudwell's wharf on the River Welland in 1914. Timber and full sacks are being transferred between a barge and the light railway using a horse worked crane. (Stewart Squires via E Sismey)

Figure 3.2
In the 1930s the coaster Castlerock was a regular visitor to George Caudwell's wharf. The ship would bring fertiliser from the London Docks or seed potatoes from Scotland.
(Stewart Squires via E Sismey)

when the firm agreed to lay the line for a one year trial. At the end of this he would either pay to retain it or they would remove it free of charge.

It was a success and was the precursor of over 140 miles of line laid and operated on over fifty Lincolnshire farms from 1909 through to 1969[4]. They were used in other counties as well but not to the extent they were in Lincolnshire *(Chapter 3.1)*. On heavy land in winter four horses could be needed to haul one cart loaded with five tons of potatoes out of a field. Using a railway, one horse could haul six tons on its own. Furthermore, the equipment was lightweight and could be laid, moved and maintained by the existing farm labour. Horses were the most common motive power but the longer lines also used lightweight locomotives, almost all with internal combustion engines, similar to the engines used to power tractors which were also increasingly being introduced to farms in the first half of the twentieth century. In 1930 George Caudwell purchased a Hudson locomotive for the Wraggmarsh House railway.

Wraggmarsh House Farm also lay conveniently alongside the River Welland on which he built his own wharf, also linked to his light railway, and two small barges to operate from it *(Figure 3.1)*. A larger wharf followed in 1915 with a steam crane to replace the earlier, horse worked, crane. A small steam tug and three barges replaced the first barges. Loads of up to 80 tons at a time were carried. Corn, peas and potatoes were taken to Boston and Kings Lynn and seed potatoes and fertiliser brought back. The wharf was also visited by small coasters bring seed potatoes direct from Scotland *(Figure 3.2)*.

Narrow gauge railways were also laid for the potato crops on Fen and Marsh farms in Lincolnshire that George and other members of the Caudwell family owned. These were at Dawsmere, Grainthorpe, Holbeach St Marks, Holbeach St Matthews, Marshchapel, North Somercotes, Tetney and Weston.

George Caudwell has at least one other claim to fame. On the 2 August 1926 a Major Savage dusted forty acres of *Majestic* potatoes in twenty-five minutes, the first use of an aircraft for aerial crop spraying in the United Kingdom[5].

William Dennis
William Dennis was born in 1841 in Horsington, near Horncastle in Lincolnshire. At the age of twenty he arrived in Kirton to find employment on a local farm. He then worked for a potato merchant before starting to grow and sell potatoes on his own account. In 1871 he bought his first six acres of land in Kirton. In the 1880s he took advantage of a time when large farms were difficult to let and for men with the capital there were opportunities to build up a substantial business[6]. His acreage was to expand to 5000 acres in Kirton and in other parts of Lincolnshire by 1907 and to some

12,000 acres in 1918, the latter including 2000 acres in the Kirton area together with another 2000 acres at Deeping St Nicholas and 8000 acres at Nocton[7]. In 1919 William Dennis and Sons became a limited company with a share capital of nearly £2 million. This became a trend in the 1930s as more large farms became corporate businesses.[8]

In the early part of the twentieth century some 1500 acres, around one third of his landholding here, was used to grow potatoes. Astute in the use of publicity to promote his business, in February 1899 he gave a 'potato tea' in Kirton for those who had helped with the potato harvest[9]. On a grander scale, in 1902, at a cost of £1000 he gave all the potatoes consumed at a dinner given to London's poor to celebrate the Coronation of Edward VII.[10] It was for reasons such as this that William Dennis became known as the Potato King.

Figure 3.3
The statue of William Dennis, 1841 – 1924, erected in front of Kirton Town Hall in 1930.
(Stewart Squires)

William Dennis lived in Kirton, at Kirton House. With his wife he had five sons and four daughters, the sons all joining him in the business. Their roles are interesting for what they tell about the influence of the family. John looked after their interests in London, at Kings Cross and Covent Garden. He was Mayor of the City of Westminster in 1907/8 and a Conservative MP 1918-22. During the First World War he was Potato Controller at the Ministry of Food; Joe managed the branches at Ramsey, Leicester and Jersey; James lived at Frampton Hall and managed the local estate; Tom travelled abroad for the firm before settling in Kirton in 1904; Frank also lived in Kirton, with a management role that saw him active in land drainage matters. He was also a successful racehorse owner and breeder.

William Dennis also took a great interest in local affairs. He sponsored the Kirton Brass Band. A staunch Methodist, in 1902 he paid for the completion of the Wesleyan Methodist Chapel, opened by his wife in November 1902. In 1911 he presented Kirton Town Hall to the village. Fund raising for the land was by local people, efforts including a book of favourite recipes to which he made up the shortfall of £150. The Hall cost £1000 and was officially opened 29 August 1912.

In 1930, following his death in 1924, a statue to his memory was erected in front of the Town Hall. William Dennis is shown as a bronze figure, seated on top of a Portland stone plinth *(Figure 3.3)*. The front panel is inscribed simply 'WILLIAM DENNIS 1841-1924'. The other three panels record in fine detail the three great interests of his working life, the drainage of the land, the growing of wheat and the cultivation of potatoes. These reflect the saying for which he was noted and which was a statement of his farming philosophy. 'Plough deep, till the soil, plant good seed, manure liberally, but first get the water off your land.'

John Arthur Godfrey, Ralph Jacques Godfrey, and Arthur Eric Godfrey

J. Arthur Godfrey was born in 1874 *(Figure 3.4)* and in the 1890s farmed a small farm at East Butterwick.

Figure 3.4
J Arthur Godfrey,
1874 – 1948.
(Courtesy of Jim Godfrey)

Figure 3.5
Ralph Jaques Godfrey,
1901 – 1968.
(Courtesy of Jim Godfrey)

In 1911 W. Dennis & Sons Ltd bought the 1100 acre West Butterwick Estate by the river Trent in North Lincolnshire from the Sheffield family and formed a company, Dennis and Godfrey, to farm 900 acres of this estate. The company was owned 90% by Dennis and 10% by Godfrey.[11]

When the Dennis family sold out to Agricultural Industries in 1926 Arthur Godfrey bought the 110 acre Hall Farm, West Butterwick. His sons Ralph, born in 1900 *(Figure 3.5)* and Eric, born in 1908, *(Figure 3.6)* were by this time farming on their own account in the Trent and Don valleys having learnt their potato growing from the Dennis family. Ralph rented the 140 acre Burringham South Grange in 1919 and his first potato crop yielded fourteen tons per acre and sold for £10 per ton, a very profitable year. This is in contrast to his nephew Jim who sold his first potato crop in 1974 at £10 per ton, a poor year for potato growers.

During the depression years of the 1920s and 1930s potatoes were more profitable than wheat so they grew potatoes one year in three. However, this led to potato cyst nematodes (eelworm) becoming a prevalent pest and in 1932 Ralph rented a farm on the Lincolnshire Wolds at Melton Ross from Lord Yarborough to widen his potato rotation. Ralph was one of the first farmers in the area to recognise the devastating impact of this pest. This stony land had never grown potatoes and was thus free of eelworm so this opened up new opportunities, although many of his new neighbours were sceptical. Arthur and his two sons continued to expand taking more farms on the Lincolnshire Wolds and at Sunk Island in East Yorkshire and when Arthur died in 1948 they were growing over 1300 acres of potatoes.

The main variety grown in the inter war years and up to the 1960s was *Majestic*, sold in Manchester and other cities in Lancashire and Yorkshire, mainly for the fish and chip trade. In the early years the crop was taken by rail direct to these markets; however in the 1950s road haulage took over as the main transport to market.

In 1940 Ralph was persuaded by the Ministry of Agriculture to chair one of the War Agricultural Executive Committees. This resulted in the ploughing up of considerable areas of land, notably 3000 acres on the Lincolnshire and Nottinghamshire border, in the Epworth and Gringley areas, of variable quality land, to help increase the country's food supply.

Ralph's success as a potato grower was down to detail. On one occasion at his Eastoft Grange farm he was unhappy with the spacing of the hand planted seed potatoes so he instructed the gang to pick up all the seed potatoes and replant them at the correct spacing. This action ensured all his farm foremen on his other farms paid attention to detail. In later years he developed a wheeled dibber to ensure accuracy of planting. He was also a pioneer on the use of basic slag from the steelworks at Scunthorpe as a source of phosphate fertiliser.

The Godfrey farming business continued with Eric's two sons, John and Jim joining the business in the early 1970s, and in 1986 they purchased a farm in the prime potato growing area of Holbeach Marsh. Jim's interest in potatoes went beyond the farm and he was chairman of the Potato Marketing Board, the Scottish Crop Research Institute and the International Potato Centre in Peru. Jim's two sons Alex and Sam joined the business in 2008 thus ensuring succession. The business grows a smaller area of potatoes today on a wider rotation mainly supplying the multiple retailers.

Clifford Nicholson

Clifford Nicholson was born in 1892 at Willoughton Manor, near Gainsborough. He was the son of a landowner who also farmed land at Scotter, Scotton, Hibaldstow and Broughton. At the age of nineteen he went to work on an estate of some 2200 acres at Riby in the Lincolnshire Wolds and was quickly given the responsibility to manage it. Here he developed an interest in sheep breeding before moving on to a farm his father bought for him at Horkstow.

Figure 3.6
Arthur Eric Godfrey, 1908 – 1991.
(Courtesy of Jim Godfrey)

In the First World War he served in the Life Guards, and he married in 1917. After the War he set himself three ambitions: to win all the first prizes at the Royal Show in the Lincoln Longwool classes; to restore the family estate to the size it had been in his grandfather's day; and to win the Grand National.

The first of the three was achieved very quickly, in 1919. The second occupied much of his time in the interwar period. At a time of recession land was cheap. By 1939 he owned some 9500 acres, increased to 32,000 acres by 1969. 18,000 acres of this was in South Africa and was built up in an enduring business partnership with John Rowles.

Interested in racing and breeding horses from an early age, it was in the early 1930s that he took this up seriously and set up his racing stables at Willoughton. He owned many successful horses but despite this did not manage to win the Grand National. One of his successful horses was named Limestone Edward which ran in the 1946 Grand National, finishing in sixth place *(Figure 3.7)*. Limestone figured highly in his life, farming on limestone land, having a company named the Limestone Farming Company and building walls and buildings in the Willoughton area from the stone. As far as potatoes were concerned he made a success of growing *King Edwards* which he called *Limestone Edwards*, hence he named a racehorse after a potato.

Figure 3.7
Clifford Nicholson with Limestone Edward, his horse which came in sixth place in the 1946 Grand National.
(Courtesy of Graham Rowles Nicholson)

In 1964 he was one of the founders of what is now the Injured Jockeys Fund and one of its first Trustees.

As is clear from the references in *Chapters 2 and 5*, stony soils can create problems for the lifting of a potato crop free from damage and blemishes. Clifford Nicholson showed that this could be done. He was an early pioneer of chitting potatoes under glass prior to their planting out *(see Chapter 2)*, and also continued the tradition of Lincolnshire growers supplying the Liverpool and Manchester areas. He used road transport rather than rail.

Clifford Nicholson died in 1972 but his companies continue to flourish today both in Lincolnshire and South Africa. Indeed, in 2010 the South African estate managers were awarded the accolade of 'Seed Potato Farmer of the Year' for the whole of South Africa.

The information for this biographical note came from family records and a conversation with **Graham Rowles Nicholson**, to whom I am very grateful.

Sir Joseph Nickerson
Sir Joseph Nickerson was not only a Lincolnshire farmer but also one of the most progressive and innovative

Figure 3.8
Sir Joseph Nickerson on Wemmergill Moor, Co. Durham, on which he shot grouse for over 40 years.
(Courtesy of Nickerson Research Centre)

agriculturalists of the last half of the twentieth century *(Figure 3.8)*. Born in 1914, in the 1930s he managed, on behalf of his father, an ever increasing estate around Rothwell in north Lincolnshire.

It was in the late 1940s that he began to campaign for the introduction of plant breeders' legislation in the United Kingdom. This led to the establishment of Nickerson Rothwell Plant Breeders Ltd, one of the largest private plant breeding operations in Europe. Trials were always underway at Rothwell but increasingly in Europe and then elsewhere in the world. Many new and improved varieties of seeds were developed and played a major role in the increase of crop yields through the 1960s and 1970s.

Cherry Valley Farms was established in 1960 to produce ducks. It quickly became the largest supplier of oven ready ducks in Britain and, from 1981, became increasingly influential in China and the Far East.

The Cotswold Pig Company was acquired in 1970 and, in common with Sir Joseph's other interests, quickly became influential in pig breeding and development.

It was in the late 1950s that Sir Joseph became involved with the seed potato industry. In 1958 twenty-five tons of a Dutch variety, *Sirtema*, were imported and planted in trials at Rothwell and on another farm in Yorkshire. They did well and the following year he applied to import another twenty-five tons. This was refused and the Company were advised that their previous licence had been issued in error. Strict controls to prevent the spread of disease severely limited the amount of seed potatoes that could be imported and then they could only be trialled indoors. However, small quantities of another variety had also been imported and grown on farms in Aberdeenshire and Northern Ireland and these were developed to become the popular *Désirée.*

Because of the regulations that had proved such a problem in these early days much of the trialling and development of seed potatoes up to the mid 1960s was carried out on the Isle of Man.

As a very well known sportsman and naturalist, Sir Joseph changed the landscape around Rothwell with the planting of trees in small woodlands and shelter belts. His field hedgerows were maintained in a very distinctive tall and thick 'A' shape. He also served on the Caistor Rural District Council and was involved with several agricultural organisations. He was knighted in 1983 for services to agriculture, and he died in 1990.

See also Ralph Whitlock, *Roots in the Soil, an Adventure in Agriculture,* Plas Enterprises, Hertford, 1987.

Charles Sharpe

Charles Sharpe senior established his business as a nurseryman in Sleaford in the early nineteenth century. A map of the town of 1849 shows the location of the nursery along the south side of what is now Boston Road, the site of the present playing fields.

After his death his son, also Charles Sharpe, evolved the business into that of a seed merchant, at first serving local needs but developing it to the extent that he was supplying the whole of the United Kingdom as well as North America, Germany and France.[12] In 1868 he led a national movement to improve standards in the trade and was largely responsible for the Adulteration of Seeds Bill introduced in 1869.[13]

He lived in Boston Road in a large house built adjacent to one of several warehouses in the town, some of them rail connected.

The firm supplied seed potatoes, including two varieties which they introduced in 1891 and were named after them, *Sharpe's Victor*[14] and *Sharpe's Pink Seedling. Sharpe's Express*, which is still popular today, followed in 1901. However, the supply of seed potatoes was never one of their mainstream activities; they were known more for swedes, turnips, sugar beet and peas.

Charles Sharpe died on 11 May 1897, aged sixty-seven, and is buried at Quarrington Church.

A. H. Worth

Arthur Hovenden Worth was born on a farm, Strawberry Hall, Tydd St Mary, near Wisbech, in 1877 although the family originated in Bourne, Lincolnshire. His middle name has a family connection, the details of which are lost in the mists

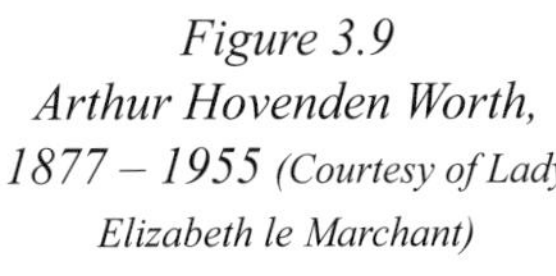

Figure 3.9
Arthur Hovenden Worth, 1877 – 1955 (Courtesy of Lady Elizabeth le Marchant)

Figure 3.10
The loading dock of the Fleet Light Railway at Fleet Station, about 1920. In the foreground are bagged potatoes being transferred into railway wagons in a siding off the Midland and Great Northern Joint Railway. *(Stewart Squires via David Spain)*

of time. Arthur's father, Thomas Mordaunt, settled in Lutton Marsh in south Lincolnshire in about 1892. In 1900 Arthur married Lizzie Thompson, whose father farmed adjacent land in Lutton Marsh, and with whom he had five children.

With the help of his father, he purchased 1500 acres of land at Holbeach Hurn, extended by an additional 500 acres shortly after. He ploughed what was then largely grassland to grow potatoes, cereals and clover leys for grazing livestock. Mustard was also grown as a catch crop, for Colman's of Norwich. An entrepreneur as well as a farmer, he was influential not only in the development of the potato industry but also in the growing of celery (also as a catch crop) where he was the first to grow a self blanching variety. He also purchased other farms, mostly within Lincolnshire, to set his children up in farming.

Potatoes are the crop for which he is best known and the principal crop of the family firm which is his legacy today. With the cooperation of Grattons, machinery manufacturers of Boston, he invented a horse drawn dusting machine for the application of a special Bordeaux/copper powder mixture for the control of potato blight.[15] Control of disease was very important to the extent that all the farm workers were provided with free potatoes as they were not allowed to grow them within their own gardens, not only because of the blight problem, but also to prevent the spread of viruses. He also introduced mechanisation, in the form of light railways, in a very big way.

We have seen already in the notes on George Caudwell above that the latter was the man who revolutionised farm transport with the introduction of a narrow gauge railway. In 1909 Arthur Worth took this a stage further and built not only a railway serving his fields and farmsteads, and incidentally the adjacent farms of his father-in-law at Dawsmere, but also to provide a link with his nearest railway station, at Fleet, two and a half miles to the south.[16] Here was a large loading dock and exchange sidings to enable seeds and fertilisers to be brought in and farm produce taken away. It has been said that the railway and its equipment cost some £10,000 and this was a considerable investment at that time. The line developed to some thirteen miles in extent, excluding an additional seven miles on the Thompson's farms at Dawsmere. These Dawsmere farms were owned by his wife's family, hence the physical railway link as well as a strong family link.

Most farm railways were relatively short and relied on horses to provide the motive power. Arthur Worth's railway was so large that locomotives were introduced from 1923. The use of the railway was so successful that railways were also built on other farms that members of the family owned, for example at Christie House Farm, Holbeach St Matthew; Havenhouse near Skegness in 1927 and at Hasse and Mettleham Farms, Soham, near Ely.

During World War I Arthur Worth was recruited to maximise home grown food production with the aim of reducing the amount of imported food. He was eventually managing some 12,000 acres of land, spending a significant amount of time travelling on horseback or pony and trap to achieve this.

Although he was an early user of tractors, some being purchased prior to World War II, the farms used many horses and he was an enthusiastic shower of the Suffolk Punch breed.

Hovenden House, with its associated small park, was built for A.H. Worth in 1911, in the countryside north of Fleet Hargate.[17] The architect J.E. Dixon-Spain designed the house, one of the last country houses to be built in

Lincolnshire before that great culling of the country house began after 1919. A. H. Worth was a man who loved his garden, and he designed both the gardens and park associated with his new home. Hovenden House is now a Cheshire Home.

In the 1920s he provided his own sacks displaying his own monogram (BCM/LNCS), to be recognised easily by dealers and customers as a mark of the quality of the potatoes he produced.

He was an early car owner and always drove himself, although he travelled around the farm on horseback and also visited places such as Holbeach and Spalding by pony and trap. Country sports were his great interest. Holidays were taken in Scotland for trout and salmon fishing and in the inter war period he rented space at the stables at Belton House from where he enjoyed hunting. He also shot and hosted shooting parties on his land on Holbeach Marsh. Literature was another interest, especially Shakespeare and Walter Scott. He was also a JP for the South Holland District.[18]

About five years before he died he left to live in retirement near Oakham. He died in 1955, pre-deceasing his wife by three days. He was remembered as a trustworthy and self effacing man with a great concern for people. A plaque in his memory can be seen in the Church of St Luke at Holbeach Hurn.

The information for this biographical note came largely from conversations with **Lady Elizabeth le Marchant**, his daughter, and **Tony Worth**, his grandson, to whom I am very grateful.

Endnotes

1 Jonathan Brown, *Farming in Lincolnshire 1850-1945*, History of Lincolnshire Committee, (Lincoln 2005), p.56-57.

2 www.soilandhealth.org/01library/010115darwin/fvm.intro.howard.html

3 Stewart E Squires, *The Lincolnshire Potato Railways*, Second revised edition, (Usk 2005), p.23.

4 Stewart E Squires, *The Lincolnshire Potato Railways*, p.25.

5 RAF Museum, Cosford. Milestones of Flight.

6 Jonathan Brown, *Farming in Lincolnshire 1850-1945*, p.58.

7 Stewart E Squires, *The Lincolnshire Potato Railways*, Second Revised Edition, (Usk 2005), p.24-25, and see also The Kirton Book Group, *Kirton in Holland*, 1990.

8 Jonathan Brown, *Farming in Lincolnshire 1850-1945*, History of Lincolnshire Committee, 2005, p.31.

9 The Kirton Book Group, *Kirton in Holland*, (Kirton 1990), p.24.

10 Ruby Hunt, Portrait of a Village; Kirton, *Lincolnshire Life*, February 1969, p.45-49.

11 Stewart E Squires, *The Lincolnshire Potato Railways*, p.30, 32-33, 35.

12 Simon Pawley, *The Book of Sleaford,* Barron Birch, 1996.

13 Neil R Wright, *Lincolnshire Towns and Industry 1700 – 1914,* History of Lincolnshire Committee Volume XI, 1982.

14 Jonathan Brown, *Farming in Lincolnshire 1850-1945*, History of Lincolnshire Committee, 2005.

15 QV Foods publicity leaflet, Worths Farms website.

16 Stewart E Squires, *The Lincolnshire Potato Railways*, Second Revised Edition, (Usk 2005), p.105-115.

17 Nikolaus Pevsner and John Harris, *The Buildings of England, Lincolnshire*, Penguin Books, Second Edition, (1989), p.281.

18 Kelly's *Directory of Lincolnshire*, 1937.

3.1 SACK HIRE AND THE RAILWAYS

Stewart Squires

The transport of grain, peas and potatoes required a vast number of sacks. One relatively little known activity of the railway companies was the hire of hessian sacks to farmers. Initially, this was done by private companies and there were many within the county. Indeed, sack supply companies survived right up to the end of transportation, using sacks in the middle of the twentieth century.

In Lincolnshire one such, the Railway Sack Owning Company, with its headquarters in Boston, served the needs of the customers of the Great Northern Railway.[1] The latter were the first railway company to take on sack hire themselves when, on 1 July 1876, they took over this particular business. Railway companies, because of their network of staff at rural stations, were in a better position to trace and secure the return of sacks after hire and send out the accounts quickly, and most railway companies nationwide soon followed suit.

Figure 3.1.1
The former Boston Sack Depot in commercial use, 1995.
(Stewart Squires)

Sack hire was part of a chain of services to meet the needs of farmers. This included a collection and delivery service, the provision of rail served warehouses, regular goods trains, express if need be for perishable goods, rail-served markets, as well as telephones at rural stations at a time when few private houses had them.

In 1923, when the grouping of railway companies into regional organisations took place, the Sack Departments of the Great Northern, Great Eastern and Great Central Railways were amalgamated and the existing sack depots at Boston *(Figure 3.1.1)*, Ely and Grimsby Docks were closed. The whole of the sack business was concentrated in Lincoln. This depot was responsible for distributing sacks throughout the network, receiving empty sacks on return, making repairs and rendering all accounts. The London and North Eastern Railway sack depots in 1939 were in Aberdeen, Edinburgh, York and Lincoln. Between them they had approximately 3,000,000 sacks

Figure 3.1.2
A view of the Lincoln Sack Depot with stacked sacks, and a few laid out to dry in the sun. Taken immediately before closure, July 1963.
(Society for Lincolnshire History and Archaeology, via the late Mick Quixley)

for hire, half of these from the Southern Area based in Lincoln.[2]

The Lincoln depot was established in what had been the Great Central Railway Goods and Grain Warehouse. The warehouse was opened as a new building on 8 July1907,[3] adjacent to the Ropewalk and alongside the Lincoln Engine Shed. Surplus to requirements after the grouping its size and siding connections made it ideal for its new purpose. *(Figure 3.1.2)*

Farmers would order the sacks they needed from their local station. They came in units of twenty, with one sack containing nineteen others. When filled they were returned to the station for despatch. As the ownership of the potatoes changed so did the responsibility for paying the hire charge. Sacks were so useful on the farm that farmers would often try to keep some, but lost sacks had to be paid for. Station clerks had the responsibility for dealing with outstanding accounts and the clerk for Habrough and Stallingborough stations recorded in 1941 that this work involved several days a month cycling around the farms or visiting them with the station delivery lorry on its rounds.[4]

Figure 3.1.3
Lincoln University Library today.
(Stewart Squires)

The Lincoln Sack Depot employed a large number of women. Their job was to sort through the returned sacks, clean and make repairs when necessary, using patches taken from those in the worst condition and stack them ready to be sent out again. It was a dusty and dirty job with rats and mice everywhere.[5]

The Lincoln Sack Depot closed in 1963. The building was sold in 1967 to become Harcros Builders Merchants. Today it has become the Library for the University of Lincoln, albeit shorn of its extensive covered platforms to the east. *(Figure 3.1.3)* The Boston Sack Depot also still survives as a commercial unit on what is now the Redstone Industrial Estate.

Endnotes

1 E H Owen, *Railway Grain Sacks* in *London and North Eastern Railway Magazine,* Vol 29, No 9, September 1939, p.503.

2 E H Owen, Ibid.

3 J G Ruddock and R E Pearson, *The Railway History of Lincoln,* J G Ruddock and Partners, (Lincoln 1974) p.227.

4 N L Davison, *My Days Work* in *London and North Eastern Railway Magazine,* Vol 31, No 3, March 1941, p.66.

5 'The not so good old days', *Lincolnshire Echo*, Wednesday 11 February 1998, p.6.

3.2 THE GREAT POTATO BOOM

Dennis Mills

Figure 3.2.1
Advert for Titus Kime's business
(Courtesy of Dennis Mills)

"ELDORADO."

"ELDORADO" is not a new Potato. It was sent out by ——— amongst the "Evergood" some years ago, and therefore, because it is not new, it is not worth the exorbitant prices being charged for it, and I release all my customers from their purchases of this Potato and will return all deposits.

T. KIME, MAREHAM-LE-FEN, BOSTON, Lincolnshire.

Figure 3.2.2
Titus Kime's announcement about 'Eldorado'
(Courtesy of Dennis Mills)

Like most booms, the Great Potato Boom worked up gradually, and the date 1904 marks the crash at the end. The boom came about partly because of the way in which enough seed potatoes of a new variety are created to meet demand quickly in a very competitive market. For the maincrop varieties, yield was the critical factor, although taste and conformation were also taken into consideration. When six tons an acre was regarded as a good crop, the prospect of ten tons was extremely attractive.

As anyone who has planted a few rows of potatoes in his back garden can testify, it is worth keeping seed potatoes somewhere where they can 'chit', that is, develop sprouts from which the plant will grow. If there are several sprouts on a seed potato, by cutting up this tuber, it is possible, as it were, to produce several seed potatoes, say three, that will all grow independently. As a healthy plant might produce, say, ten to twenty potatoes of mature size by the time they are

Figure 3.2.3
At the height of the 'potato boom' in 1902, the profit from just four acres of Mr Findlay's variety Up-to-Date enabled a farmer in Freiston to build a new house, which was named after the potato variety. (Adrian White)

harvested, one whole seed potato with three sprouts might yield forty to sixty at harvest time. This is the basis on which large increases in available seed could be obtained within a single season. A boom could develop from the race to produce seed quickly, as well as in the sales of new well-favoured potatoes to the public.

Most of this account is based on the publications of Titus Kime of Mareham-le-Fen, a potato grower and seed potato grower and merchant *(Figure 3.2.1)*, together with newspaper reports and stories handed down to the writer by Harry Major, his maternal grandfather, who was one of Kime's work people.[1] To demonstrate the gradual build-up of the boom, Kime began the story in 1892-93 when Mr A. Findlay of Auchtermuchty in Fifeshire brought out *Up-to-Date*,[2] which was so favourably received that growers could get £10 a ton for it, when £2-3 a ton was the normal farm gate price for eating potatoes, £3-4 for seed. *(Figures 3.2.3 and 3.2.4)* In 1894-95 Findlay introduced *Challenge*, for which the demand was so great that he sold no more than a single stone to any one buyer at one shilling a pound (14 shillings a stone) or the equivalent of £112 a ton. Kime explained that from a single stone of seed, owing to the multiplier effect, a good grower could produce enough seed to plant 10 acres within three years, and 'nearly a county' after four years. In 1896 Kime sold *Challenge* seed for £40 a ton, enough to plant an acre. This was a fall on the previous year as more seed was

Figure 3.2.4
The decorative cast iron plaque on the house giving the name and date. (Adrian White)

available, but at 10 tons to the acre the return could be £400, or four times what *Up-to-Date* had been bringing in two or three years earlier.

And so the boom moved on with Findlay producing a string of new varieties. In 1903 the price of *Eldorado*, which Findlay had introduced the year before, was £3-5,000 a ton, or three to five times the price of *Northern Star* in 1900. However, not all of Findlay's new offers had been tested properly for consistency of character and yield, and freedom from disease. It was possible to 'force' a trial variety with unfortunate effects. Whether he was downright dishonest, or *Eldorado* had simply not been tested well enough for consistency, will probably never be known (*Figure 3.2.2*).

However, Kime had his suspicions, and in 1904 asked Harry Major to plant a few *Eldorados* in his cottage garden and keep quiet about them. In early July Harry and Kime lifted these potatoes and discovered that they were 'not a new Potato', whereupon Kime put advertisements to this effect in three Lincolnshire newspapers. This caused tremendous confusion and anger (against Kime as well as Findlay) amongst potato growers and other seed merchants, although the boom did not burst immediately. In November Findlay took Kime to court for libel and sued for £20,000 damages, probably enough to ruin even a prosperous man like Kime. The case fell through and it became accepted that Findlay had misled customers by selling *Eldorado* mixed with either *Northern Star* or *Evergood*, which shared some of *Eldorado's* characteristics. One of the consequences of the boom's crash was the formation of the National Potato Society, with the intention of regulating the trade.

Endnotes

1 Dennis Mills, *'Titus Kime, Entrepreneur of Mareham-le-Fen, 1848-1931, and the Eldorado Potato Boom of 1903-04'*, pp.139-50, especially, pp.144-149, in Jean Howard and David Start (eds.), *All Things Lincolnshire*, Lincoln, Society for Lincolnshire History and Archaeology, 2007.

2 The editors are grateful to Nigel Marshall of Frieston for bringing to our attention the *Up-to-Date* house illustrated in Figures 3.2.3 & 3.2.4 and to the owner for allowing the house to be photographed.

Chapter 4

TATEY PICKING TIME

Abigail Hunt

Introduction

This chapter relates the experiences of child, female, and migrant labourers working with potato crops in Lincolnshire between 1850 and 1960. Between those dates the labourer was crucial to the running of the farm in Lincolnshire, although the need for workers slowly decreased throughout the nineteenth and twentieth centuries as 'the progress of machinery helped farmers to dispense with the need for extra hands'. It is often assumed that this agricultural workforce consisted 'almost exclusively of male adults'[1] but in reality this was far from the case. During the nineteenth and twentieth centuries women and children were an important and major part of the labour force, often undertaking the most unpleasant types of agricultural labour. The groups of men that were employed were not always local but gangs of migrant labourers particularly from Ireland. Potato crops, for which the county was renowned, formed one of the main constituents of work for these three groups of people.

This chapter of the book does not just recount the role of child, female, and migrant workers in the growing and harvesting of the potato crop, but attempts to examine their experiences to re-present this aspect of Lincolnshire's history. Due to the wealth of material available the chapter is based on the hundred or so years between 1850 and 1960, a period of relative continuity in Lincolnshire's agricultural and rural history. Wherever possible oral testimonies collected as part of a county-wide research project in 2007 are used to provide an individual and highly personal perspective on this aspect of Lincolnshire's agricultural past. This piece is based on a wider PhD research project carried out between 2003 and 2011 for the University of Lincoln which examined changes in agricultural practice in Lincolnshire, the impact on rural culture, and its representation in the county's museums.

Child Labour

Today in Britain child labour is considered abhorrent and abusive. However, in the past, and actually until relatively recently, attitudes to children being part of

Figure 4.1

Potato Harvest, 1878 by J.W. Macbeth, engraved by A. Beillet.

(Courtesy Royal Academy)

Figure 4.2
Potato picking 'gang' of women and children, at William 'Sugar' Jacklin's farm.
(MLL8740, from the Illustrations Index courtesy of Lincolnshire County Council)

the labour force were different, for example the *Boston Standard* History and Nostalgia pages, available on line, feature a snippet from the news of April 25th 1942 when it was reported that:

> Holland County Council's education committee met to discuss child labour on the farms, and Coun E.E. Welby-Everard said that due to the 'extreme acuteness of labour shortage on the land' it would not be a 'wholly bad thing' for 12 to 14-year-olds to work harder and longer.[2]

This was of course wartime and therefore the comments may have been driven by the special requirements of these extraordinary times, but they may also be indicative of the attitudes, at least in rural Lincolnshire, to child labour in the early to mid-twentieth century.

Gang Labour

One of the ways in which large numbers of children were employed to work on the land in Lincolnshire during the nineteenth century was as part of the gang system.

Gang labour had existed before the introduction of the New Poor Law in 1834, but a large increase in the employment of women and children in agriculture was witnessed after its adoption, as they had to contribute to the household income to avoid the severe consequences of poverty.[3] By the 1850s it was a prevalent system of employment, and dominated by women and children workers, who undertook the worst types of agricultural labour. In the fenlands of the county they worked as day labourers, employed on the 'roughest, if not the heaviest, classes of work'.[4] *(Figures 4.1, 4.2, 4.3)*

There were, of course, several benefits for a farmer in employing gang labour: he only had to pay for labour when he required it and did not have to retain workers; it saved him the expense of housing his workers; and women and children were cheaper to employ than men as they received lower rates of pay.[5]

As the twentieth century progressed and the school leaving age was gradually raised gangs of children became less common. However, between 1943 and 1950 there was a shortage of labour due to war, and large numbers of well-organised groups, or gangs, of school children were brought into key agricultural operations, especially at harvest times. In 1943 over 1000 Farm camps were set up across the country for school children and adult volunteers that combined a country holiday with farm work in a bid to 'attract 150 – 200,000 adult workers and in excess of 300,000 children'[6] needed to bring in the various harvests during the War, and in 1944 school children in 'Nottinghamshire, Leicestershire and Lincolnshire were granted extra leave [from school]...

to assist with potato picking'.[7] Two participants in the oral history project recalled being allowed time off from school to work on local farms. Mrs Higham went to Spalding High School in the 1940s and recalled that:

> We used to have our holidays split. We didn't have the six weeks at once in the August, we had a fortnight or three weeks in October to help the farmers to get the harvest in, and we weren't working for our own parents. Then we'd help other farmers and as you were teenagers they used to give you two to a row. One picked one side and one picked the other, and you had these big wicker baskets and they used to take 'em and empty 'em, you know, in the horse and cart.

Nearly seventy miles away towards the north east of the county, in the early 1950s Mr. Snell, another grammar school pupil, engaged in similar work:

> In my time at Caistor Grammar school they allowed those people who wanted to, to get in a lorry and do potato picking for a couple of weeks. Instead of doing your lessons you had the choice. This was the 1950s and they would lorry us out from Caistor Market Place to a farm at North Kelsey[8] and we would do potato picking.

The timing of this experience is quite interesting as general historical information suggests that the labour scheme involving schoolchildren was officially discontinued by the government in 1950. Mr Snell also recalled working in a gang proper during the 1950s to pick peas.

Employees and Family Labourers

Children also worked as individuals as part of the seasonal rural labour force during the nineteenth, and well into the twentieth century, and it was accepted that the 'peak period for children's labour in the rural areas was May to September (inclusive)'.[9] During the nineteenth century 'nearly 5500 agricultural labourers were aged from five to nine', [10] and by the time most children were in their early teens they left school to take up work full time. It is estimated that during the 1860s little more than half the children in the country

Figure 4.3
Potato gang of men, women and children with two horses, Old Leake area.
(Courtesy of the White family, Old Leake)

Figure 4.4
Three men riddling and bagging up potatoes, Smith's Potato Estates, Nocton
(LC9948 from the Illustrations Index courtesy of Lincolnshire County Council)

were receiving an education, which prompted the Acts referred to earlier, including the Agricultural Children Act. However, this Act still allowed country children between the ages of eight and ten to work during the harvest, and after the age of ten they were allowed to be released further for farm work provided they attended school for a particular number of days a year. This did lead to a reduction in the number of children working on farms as the century closed, but late nineteenth century and early twentieth century schooling was affected by this rural practice of taking children out of the classroom to use them as labour and 'even when children did go to school, their attendance was spasmodic'.[11]

At the turn of the twentieth century it became less common for children to be employed as legislation was passed, pushing the legal age to work upwards. However, labour shortages both during and after the First World War meant that children were called in significant numbers to assist in agricultural labour. During the First World War children were released from school to help in the fields, and in 1917 H.A.L. Fisher claimed that 600,000 children had been released early from education during the first three years of the War, many of whom had gone into agricultural work.[12] There is evidence to suggest that this was true of Lincolnshire, with F. Moore writing:

> When we all moved to Lincolnshire just before the First World War my school career was over. I should have gone to a Lincolnshire school, but I didn't, and nobody bothered about it, and I started work.[13]

Two men, Mr Brown and Mr Bell, born in 1909 and 1907 respectively, interviewed in 2007, recounted similar experiences to that of Mr Moore directly linked to the potato crop. They both lived in South Lincolnshire, around Donington and Gosberton, after the First World War. When asked about work in the early twentieth century Mr Brown said:

> As soon as you could walk you did work. No doubt about that. Half of us didn't go to school...Quite a bit to do, especially in the tatey picking time. Mothers kept them at home to earn a bob or two. The inspector was looking round for them. Caused quite a bit of concern. Some got runned out with a brush. It was quite good.

Mr Bell added to the discussion of children at work during the early twentieth century, explaining that he left school at thirteen, c.1920, to start work. He went on to say that: 'Some left school when they were twelve.... after the First World War there were no labourers left.... there was always a job'. This sentiment was echoed by Mrs Hather who was born in 1914 and spent her early years in East Firsby, nine miles from Lincoln. She recalled her brother leaving home at twelve to work on an Uncle's farm:

> ...And I remember one of my brothers. He left home at twelve to work, go work on a farm because there was a shortage of labour because of the War.

It could be argued that children of labouring families on nineteenth and twentieth century farms, or those of families with smallholdings or farms had to work harder than any other group of children. This group were largely unseen labour, although their contributions were essential to the running of the farm. This project recorded numerous examples of children working on family farms from the beginning of the twentieth century to the 1960s across Lincolnshire.

During the lean post-World War Two years children were expected to help with a variety of jobs on their family's farm or smallholding, particularly those that required more labour; it was obviously more cost effective to use free family labour than pay external labourers. This was particularly common in areas like the south of the county where more labour-intensive crops, such as potatoes, were grown. Mrs Jackson whose father had a smallholding at Sutton Bridge remembered:

> I was one of a large brood so we had to help. Even before we left school we had to help on the land....The worst job I remember was cross harrow picking....The potatoes would be ploughed out by a horse and plough but as always some would be covered over...We had to go afterwards when it was supposedly cleared and my father would take the harrows one way and we would have to go with a basket and pick these stray ones up. It was a soul destroying job.

Much like Mrs Jackson, Mrs Higham also disliked having to help on the family farm with the potato harvest during the mid twentieth century, and during her interview she specified that she particularly 'didn't like green potato picking'.

Even children in families of larger landowners would help during this period. Mr Watts recalled his experiences of helping on one of his father's farms at Thorpe Latimer in the 1950s:

> I remember working the horses, especially when we had potato picking. I was only an old boy, but it was my job to lead the horses from the pickers to the graves.

Other children left school to work as labourers on farms; Mr Dawson started work for Dring's in Holland Fen in 1946 at the age of 15:

> When I first were there I was down riddling tates at the grave. You see that was my first job. I went in September time (*Figure 4.4*).

This work carried on through winter and Mr Dawson's wife recalled her early experiences of working through the harsh winters of the early 1960s. She remembered the state of the frozen potato graves:

> Sometimes they was that frozen in the winter time they used to put a chain and pull it off with a tractor 'cause it was that frozen. We used to stand out there, now they're complaining in a shed if it's cold you know! You'd try to warm your hands on the little motor that was on the riddler.

It would seem that throughout the period children had to work hard in all weather conditions to contribute to the family income or local economy. It would be easy to consider them an exploited workforce, but evidence was collected throughout the project to suggest that children accepted that their families required their assistance, and were often glad to leave school for a few weeks to work on the potato harvest. They could also be defiant if they did not agree with working practices they were subjected to. For instance Mrs Hayes left school at the age of 15 to work on the land in 1923 and recalled that in her first job:

> We used to set potatoes, set them out of boxes. One each end, and, the boss we worked for he insisted we walk backwards...But we used to turn round when he'd gone by.

Women

Between 1850 and 1960 women were central to the success of agriculture with their labour patterns and job roles mirroring those of children. Although it was preferable for members of polite society not to see women carrying out work, 'at the labouring level of society all women worked',[14] undertaking a wide variety of roles. It has been argued that, as the nineteenth century progressed, women worked less in the agricultural and horticultural industries, as they steadily became male dominated, but this was not the case in Lincolnshire, particularly in relation to the potato growing areas of the county.[15] In 1919 County Investigators recorded that in Lincolnshire 'year–round women's work was.... considerable in "normal times"'[16], with the majority of this work 'being concentrated in the bulb industry around Spalding and in the cultivation of potatoes in the Holland Division.'[17] *(Figure 4.5)* Census County Reports from 1921 also provide an insight into the levels of female labour in Lincolnshire at the time, with Holland in Lincolnshire being fifth in the twenty counties with the highest percentage of female to male agricultural labourers. For every eight men employed in agriculture there were fourteen women, and whilst gang labour producing potatoes will have contributed considerably to this, bulbs also account for the large percentage. By 1931 for every four men there were eleven women in Holland County reflecting declining levels of labour required due to technological innovation.[18] Mr Briggs of Holland Fen recalled that during the mid twentieth century 'there was nearly as many women as men' working on the fen.

During the nineteenth and well into the twentieth century women worked in gangs alongside men and children as day labourers *(Figure 4.6)*. Particularly busy

Figure 4.5
Women wearing sunbonnets planting potatoes.
(ML395, from the Illustrations Index courtesy Lincolnshire County Council)

times of employment for gang women were the various harvest times, although women could work year–round as 'human weed-killers, "charlocking" or picking twitch and thistles'.[19] These women were generally viewed by the middle classes as crude and vulgar because they either worked alongside men or undertook masculine work. However, as Mrs Hayes put it 'there's difference between them as there is today', suggesting that the behaviour and demeanour of these groups of women has been over generalised by commentators. Mrs Hayes could remember a few of the women she worked with being 'a little bit brazen' and relayed during her interview that it was from the women she worked with in the gangs that she learned about sex:

> I was never really explained about life and of course I used to listen to the other women, and of course, if they had been out the night before. Well you see I listened and I got to know all what they was doing.

Mrs Hayes also recalled women occasionally engaging in sexual activity whilst at work; 'and maybe you'd like see a man make his way to a barn or something and then this woman might fly off.'

Much like Mrs Hayes, Mrs Jackson also learned more about adult life from other gang women, although her experience was based more on folklore. There were no toilets in the fields when she worked in them during the 1940s and 1950s and the women would have to use the ditches at the sides of the field if they needed to relieve themselves. Some women told her that if she went to the toilet in the ditch when she was menstruating she would be attacked by a weasel; something she still remembers today.

These kinds of occurrences and behaviour meant that whilst the women who worked in the potato picking gangs of Lincolnshire were often local women in need of casual work, they had a fearsome reputation. Mr Whitten would drive gangs of women from Boston to work in the fields and stated that they were known as 'Boston Tigers', and Mr Waters recalled that the women gang workers he worked with near Lincoln would only be nice to the driver if he stopped the bus in the morning at the shop so they could buy cigarettes and chocolate. However, despite this 'rum' reputation, many interviewees provided a different image of these women. Mr Banister recalled women he worked with post World War Two near Heckington as being physically imposing due to the nature of their work, but also being very pleasant to work with:

> They were built like the, you know, proverbial brick privy, you know they, but they were lovely women, you know, don't get me wrong, I don't mean they were, but they were, but it was damned hard work.

It might be suggested that rather than being crude, some women adopted a more masculine demeanour as they were engaging in a traditionally masculine activity. Perhaps this was an unconscious expression of the traits of the role which they were performing.

It would appear that these gangs of women often comprised family groups, for example Mr Perkins stated that many of the women that came to pick potatoes on the farm he worked at in Swaton 'were sisters and aunts', and Mr Line recounted of his experience near Heckington that 'my mother and aunties had to turn out and work in the fields'. Mrs Hayes worked for her brother who was the gangmaster:

> My brother he used to have a gang and I went into his gang. We used to go all over potato picking and what-have-you.

These gangs varied in size with some participants recalling there being as many as twenty women in a group, to others that only had half a dozen or so, but all agreed it was hard work. It may be that the familiarity between the extended family groups meant that they behaved in a more relaxed manner than they might have done in another work place.

Despite a general disapproval of women working as labourers in the fields there were two occasions in the twentieth century when it was more acceptable for women to be a visible land based workforce: World Wars One and Two. Whilst these occurrences heralded new opportunities for women, academic discourse is often focussed on the tasks undertaken and the implications of equality for women in society, overlooking a key

Figure 4.6
Gang, largely of women and children, potato picking at Old Leake c. 1925. Back row from left: 2nd in patterned top: Grace Perkins (nee Faulkner); 3rd with pipe: Herbert White; 6th in similar patterned top: Dolly Faulkner (sister of Grace). Front row: 2nd from left: Charles White, aged about 14, son of Herbert.
(Courtesy of the White family, Old Leake)

question that can be asked of the period: to what extent did people's attitudes towards what work was considered acceptable for women really change? This is an important question to ask of these two periods as the historical narrative has been covered almost to the point of exhaustion, with few new perspectives offered by historians in recent years. On the surface it would appear that these two short periods are of great change, but in actuality they are not. Women had always worked on the land as labourers, but disapproval led to them being a workforce that was not spoken about or seen. It might be argued that during the two wars they are simply more visible because of a need for their labour.

Government propaganda posters from both periods portray happy, youthful and feminine women working in agriculture, suggesting a level of, or will for, public acceptance.[20] This is not an image normally presented of female field labourers. Evidence was collected of women labourers enjoying a new found freedom in the First World War in South Lincolnshire, with Mr Brown saying:

> But they used to nip through the windows at night to meet the labourers after.

This type of evidence may suggest that the First World War experience was liberating and empowering for women and that for a short period they gained some level of equality with men. However, this may be due to the desperate need to utilise them as a labour force during war time, due to the significant pressure on British farming caused by the German submarine campaign against British shipping and supply lines, the government conscripting men working in agriculture, and a lack of appreciation for how the war could disrupt agricultural systems, rather than a change in attitude.

The need for more home production combined with a lack of labour meant that women were called from all walks of life to support their country. 300,000 women labourers came from villages across the country and 16,000 from the Women's Land Army who are described as being incredibly efficient due to the 'careful selection of recruits, and supported by free transport, uniform and footwear, with a minimum wage set above the rate for village women'.[21] However, despite the lure of a decent wage many women still left the countryside to work in the cities and urban areas as urban jobs paid higher wages than agriculture, and the type of jobs were considered more socially acceptable than labouring on the land.[22]

In 1916 the County War Agricultural Committees were ordered by Central Government to register women who were willing to work on the land and put them in contact with farmers needing labour. The government also targeted middle–class women, offering them the opportunity to take part in horticultural, dairying and poultry keeping activities along with the opportunity of studying agriculture at universities.[23] Offering middle - class women the chance to participate in the more acceptable and feminine activities once again demonstrates that labouring was not fully considered acceptable and was perhaps only a suitable pursuit for working–class women.

However, after the First World War women were expected to resume their pre-war lives, and to allow men to fill their previous roles. It should be remembered that women were not granted voting rights on the same terms as men until 1928.

In 1939, at the outbreak of World War Two half the population of Britain was female and women from all walks of life were once again called upon to work on the land as young men were called up into the Services. Most of the women who came to participate in agriculture belonged to the Women's Land Army, described as 'one of the most conspicuous and memorable aspects of the food production campaign'.[24]

Whilst explored in various oral, social and local histories, the organisation is still often referred to as the 'Forgotten Army', perhaps reflecting a general disapproval of women working on the land. Indeed, the contribution of this workforce was only recently acknowledged in 2008 with the creation of a medal awarded to members of the Women's Land Army by the Department for Food and Rural Affairs (DEFRA). There are further issues in examining the contribution to agriculture by the organisation, as it was subject to government propaganda campaigns during World War Two and its representation in post war popular culture has helped propel it to mythical status, thus distorting the retelling of women's situations and experiences.[25] Current language used in the public sphere to describe the Women's Land Army and the tasks they undertook, demonstrates this issue. For example DEFRA have the following phrase on their website:

> [With their] uniform of green ties and jumpers and brown felt slouch hats, they worked from dawn to dusk each day, milking cows, digging ditches, sowing seeds and harvesting crops.[26]

What the quote fails to mention is that women also undertook unpleasant tasks such as rat catching and manure spreading. Mrs Greetham undertook a range of hard and unpleasant tasks during her service. At Ingoldsby Grange she had to pick early potatoes:

> When we got to the farm we were potato picking and it was early potatoes, and it was a back-breaking job for people that had not, sort of, been bent double like that before.

And whilst working at Donington one of her first jobs was to spread fertilizer on the land:

> Well one of my first jobs on the land was setting guano, do you call it that? For potatoes. My husband's father then had two labourers working for him, one quite old chappie and this Henry who wasn't quite so old. And I loaded the trailer with him. I went down, we were spreading guano on the land, you know, leading the horses and, you know, things like that.

Figure 4.7
Potato planting on the William Dennis Estates - Billie Brown, Mrs Sellars, Mrs Andrews, Mrs Pedlar, Mrs Young, Mrs Scrupps, Mrs Pickhall, Billie Scrupps.
(MLL8361 from the Illustrations Index courtesy Lincolnshire County Council)

Mrs Greetham lived in very basic accommodation both at Ingoldsby Grange, near Lincoln, and Swineshead, near Boston, which appears to be typical of the wartime experience. She recalled the conditions in her billet at Ingoldsby Grange and her feeling of dismay at her new accommodation:

> Feeling very weary and tired they kind of showed us our room which was heartbreaking, having no power whatsoever. Our room, bunk beds, three lots of bunk beds, we all had a little dressing table each and just two drawers, a little bit of hanging space, paraffin lighting and all that sort of thing. And naturally I thought, 17 year old, 'what have I done?'

Swineshead appears to have been just as basic from her descriptions:

> ...at the hostel in the dormitory we just had two coke fired stoves in the middle of the dormitory. And in the middle of the dining room we just had two of those, so when we got home at night the first thing we used to do was kick our boots off and sit and warm our feet...and the smell and the steam just used to go off, it was horrendous, it really was.

The reaction of farmers to their new labour source is not well recorded, but in Lincolnshire appears to have been mixed, with some farmers accepting the women, and others being exasperated by their lack of skills and training. One interviewee from Holland Fen near Boston, Mr Briggs, simply commented that the women who worked for Dennis' Farm on the Fen were: 'bloody good weren't they?'.

Traditionally it has been argued by historians that the end of the Second World War heralded a new age of equality for women, but research from the 1980s onwards has suggested that 'the wartime changes in the status of women for the main part proved to be transitory',[27] indicating that women went back to their previous occupations and it once again became frowned upon for women to work on the land after the war. In the case of Land Army Women in Lincolnshire, many returned to their previous occupations, but some remained in the area and married farmers. Several interviewees recounted this occurring in different parts of the county, with Mr. Line summarising what appears to have been the normative experience:

> Of course Land Army Girls went back to the jobs, typists or whatever they did in the cities didn't they? Some of them stayed behind and married farmers, and workers.

However, evidence collected during this research suggested that women still formed a key component of the workforce on the land. What is particularly clear from this research is that as less labour was required the numbers of women working on the land diminished, but they retained particular, or traditional, jobs on the farm. For example when mechanical potato harvesters were introduced in the 1970s women were employed to work on them sorting potatoes, something they had once done by hand.

Women were an integral part of the agricultural workforce throughout the period 1850 – 1960, especially in relation to the potato crop. They engaged in hard physical labour, especially during the potato harvest, undertaking masculine roles on the land. Despite their contribution to feeding the country, they faced general disapproval from the general public for doing this kind of work, apart from during the two world wars. They were also stereotyped as crude and vulgar because of their work, which can perhaps be attributed to the male roles and behaviours they assumed whilst at work, and unfair stereotyping of this group of women.

Migrant Workers

Perhaps the most dominant group of migrant labourers working in Lincolnshire during the period 1850–1960 was the Irish. As early as the beginning of the nineteenth century there was an influx of these workers into the county at various harvest times. Irish men would come to England to work on the corn harvests which coincided with the lull in the demand for labour in relation to potato crops in Ireland. Some were small-holders in Ireland who would use the opportunity of harvest work to pay their rent and purchase much needed supplies on their return to their homes in the winter and spring.[28]

It is difficult to comment on the number of Irish migrant workers that came to Lincolnshire during the period being examined because, although single enumeration took place in 1841, and then annually between 1880 and 1914, there is no reliable statistical information about their numbers or use.[29] There are however, comments on the figures from a national perspective which estimate that in 1841 there were around 57,651 Irish migrant workers in England and Wales, more than 70,000 in the years 1846 to 1848, 20,000 during the 1880s and 32,000 in 1900, which demonstrates the sheer numbers of workers available to Lincolnshire farmers.[30] The peaks and troughs were created by a combination of issues including increased mechanisation and less demand for labour, agricultural depression, and the effects of the Irish potato famine i.e. population decrease through death and emigration.[31] Despite falling numbers in the twentieth century due to increased mechanisation, it has been argued that the movement was still important at the time, and this research has uncovered evidence of gangs still coming to Lincolnshire annually well into the middle of the century, and in some cases until the 1970s.[32]

These workers would spread out across the country and work on circuits that followed the harvests of particular regions, Lincolnshire was part of a circuit that also included the Fens, Yorkshire, Staffordshire and Warwickshire,[33] and it has been suggested that Lincolnshire was a key meeting place for various gangs of Irish harvesters during the nineteenth century.[34] From quite early on their presence caused unease amongst the local population, and there is evidence to suggest that this would often erupt into violence. For example, in 1830 in Newton on Trent, which is situated in the north west of county, a gang of around 40 Irish workers were attacked by local men for no other reason than being 'bloody Irishmen'.[35] Collins actually describes the nineteenth century anti–Irish feeling as 'intense rivalry, to a point

Figure 4.8
Sluice Farm at Holbeach St Marks is known to have had a Paddy Hut in the 1930s and this building may have been it. The farmstead had been established in the mid nineteenth century and, between the 1905 and 1931 OS maps, a small building appeared here in the north east corner of the site. The building has been extended and altered in more recent years to serve subsequent uses but the simple form and scale of the early part, away from the camera, will be typical.
(Stewart Squires)

of open warfare, between natives and "foreigners" and the coming of the Irish was often a signal for riots and disturbances'.[36] Farmers, however, did not share the views of their labourers and were grateful for the Irish labour, recognising that 'the Lincolnshire harvest could not be gathered without their help',[37] perhaps spurred on in the knowledge that this was a convenient workforce who were 30–40% cheaper than the local labourers.[38] There is also evidence to suggest that part of their wages consisted of farm produce, as Mr Smith recounted:

> For the Irishmen we would fatten pigs up to somewhere between thirty and thirty five stone and they'd be dry cured so they'd keep for a long time…Every week when the Irishman came over for his pay he would also... part of his pay would be a joint of fat bacon.

There is little evidence of this earlier animosity towards the Irish in the twentieth century, and many participants in the oral history project discussed the groups with fondness, recalling the same gangs of men returning year upon year to work on the same farms. There was also an appreciation of how the men contributed to the local economy, with many spending their wages in the village pubs and shops. Mr Smith of Gosberton recalled that 'when they finished work in the evening and had their meal the chances are that they'd spend their night in the local pub' whilst other interviewees recounted how the majority of their wages would be spent on living expenses such as the butcher and baker who called at the farm, along with their visits to the village pub. It would appear that by the twentieth century they were an accepted part of the labour force and temporary community members.

The gangs of workers would live on the farms during their period of employment, usually in a basic outbuilding equipped with somewhere to cook, known colloquially in the south of the county at least as a 'Paddy Hut' *(Figure 4.8)*. Mr Smith of Gosberton recalled that:

> [During] my lifetime, the pre-war period and during the war we had a Paddy Hut on the farm.

This Paddy Hut was described by Mr Smith as a simple brick building that featured bunk beds and a stove for the men. The one on Mr Ashton's farm in Moulton Eaugate, which was built in 1946 was similar, a 'three roomed building with bunk beds in and a kitchen'. If there was not a hut for them to live in on the farm they would stay in the farm buildings which were again basic, and whilst one participant said they 'lived in the buildings quite happily' in Donington, another from Holland Fen described the men as having 'lived rough in the buildings'. Mr Line could remember their improvised beds in the barn on his family farm: 'potato crates with bags of chaff or bags of straw to sleep on', painting a picture of basic living conditions.

It would appear that the Irish labourers worked and played hard, were paid less than other day labourers, and lived in basic conditions whilst in Lincolnshire. It could be suggested that their repeated return to the agricultural circuit in England is not just because of a shortage of work in Ireland, but because they spent much of what they earned in the villages they stayed in. The initial animosity felt towards the Irish labour force in the nineteenth century seems to have dissipated by the twentieth century, and a genuine fondness for the workers who returned annually was demonstrated in all the oral history interviews conducted.

Summary

The three groups of workers examined in this chapter were central to the success of the potato crop in Lincolnshire: child, female, and Irish labourers all endured hard working conditions for relatively little personal gain. Without these workers the potato crops would not have been sown, harvested, and prepared for sale, yet their stories are rarely told in traditional histories of the county. This work has attempted to provide an overview of the experiences of those who worked on the Lincolnshire potato crop, using not just academic sources and historic records, but more importantly the memories of those people who worked in the fields as, or with, these labourers in a bid to redress the balance of the historical narrative.

Acknowledgements

I would like to thank the following for allowing me to record their memories and share their stories: Mrs. Higham, Cowbit; Mr. Snell, Cleethorpes; Mr. Brown, Gosberton; Mr. Bell, Gosberton; Mrs. Jackson, Long Sutton; Mr. Watts, Deeping St Nicholas; Mr. & Mrs. Dawson, Holland Fen ; Mrs. Hayes, Stickney; Mr. Banister, Heckington; Mr. Line, Heckington; Mr. Perkins, Dunsby; Mrs. Greetham, Weston; Mr. Briggs, Holland Fen; Mr. Smith, Gosberton; Mrs Hather, Market Rasen; Mr Whitten, Grimsby; Mr Waters, Lincoln; Mr Ashton, Spalding.

Endnotes

1 R. Samuel, *Village Labour in Essays in Social History*, Volume 2, Oxford, Oxford University Press, 1986, pp 79 – 97, p 93.

2 Boston Standard. *History and Nostalgia Pages*. Available from: http://www.bostonstandard.co.uk/custompages/CustomPage.aspx?PageID=66995# [Accessed 18th February 2010].

3 N. Verdon, "The Employment of Women and Children in Agriculture: A Reassessment of Agricultural Gangs in Nineteenth Century Norfolk", Agricultural History Review, 49, 1, pp 41 -55 and Orwin, C.S. and Whetham, E.H. *History of British Agriculture 1846 – 1914*, London, Longmans, Green and Co, 1964.

4 R. Samuel, *op.cit*. p. 86.

5 J.Thirsk, *English Peasant Farming: The Agrarian History of Lincolnshire from Tudor to Recent Times*, London, Routledge and Keegan Paul, 1957.

6 R.J. Moore – Colyer, "Kids in the Corn: School Harvest Camps and Farm Labour Supply in England, 1940 – 1950", *Agricultural History Review*, 52, II, 1988, pp.183-206, p.186.

7 J. Thirsk, *op.cit*. p.187.

8 Following a review of the quote used in this article Mr Snell recalled that it was in fact Howsham, a village next to North Kelsey where he went potato picking, and North Kelsey where he went pea picking.

9 B. Reay, *Microhistories, Demography, Society and Culture in Rural England 1800 – 1930*, Cambridge Studies in Population, Economy and Society in Past Time Series, Cambridge, Cambridge University Press, 1996, p.113.

10 B. Reay, *Rural Englands: Labouring Lives in the Nineteenth Century*, Hampshire, Palgrave Macmillan, 2004, p.65.

11 B. Reay, *Microhistories, Demography, Society and Culture in Rural England 1800 – 1930* (Cambridge: Cambridge University Press, 1996), p. 230.

12 A. Howkins, *Reshaping Rural England, A Social History 1850 – 1925*, London, Routledge, 1991.

13 F. Moore, and J. Hynam, *The Horses Knew the Way, Memories of a Lincolnshire Life*, Gloucs, Alan Sutton, 1991, p.29.

14 13 B. Reay Microhistories, demography, society and Culture in Rural England 1800 – 1930, Cambridge Studies in Population, Economy and Society in Past Time Series, Cambridge University Press, Cambridge, 1996, p 29.

15 G. Sturt *Change in the Village,* London, Caliban Books, 1984, p.23.

16 N. Verdon, "Agricultural Labour and the Contested Nature of Women's Work in Interwar England and Wales", *The Historical Journal*, 52, 1, 2009, pp.109-130, p.118.

17 N.Verdon, "Agricultural Labour and the Contested Nature of Women's Work in Interwar England and Wales" *The Historical Journal* 52:1 (2009), p. 118.. Also see Wallace, J.C. Farming in the Holland Division of Lincolnshire, *Agriculture The Journal of the Ministry of Agriculture*, Special Lincolnshire Number, Vol LIV, No 4, July 1947, pp. 158-165, p.163.

18 N.Verdon, "Agricultural Labour and the Contested Nature of Women's Work in Interwar England and Wales" *The Historical Journal* 52:1 (2009), pp. 109 – 130.

19 R. Samuel, *op.cit.* p 86.

20 G. Clarke, "The Women's Land Army and its Recruits 1938 – 50", *The frontline of Freedom: British Farming in the Second World War,* Eds Short, B., Watkins, C. and Martin, J.Exeter, British Agricultural History Society, 2007, pp. 101-116.

21 G. E. Mingay, *A Social History of the English Countryside*, London, Routledge, 1990, p.200.

22 A.Howkins, *The Death of Rural England: A Social History of the Countryside since 1900*, London, Routledge, 2003, p.30.

23 A. Howkins, *The Death of Rural England: A Social History of the Countryside since 1900* (London: Routledge, 2003), p.31.

24 G. Clarke, *op.cit.* p.101.

25 C. Short Watkins, J. Martin, "The Frontline of Freedom': State Led Agricultural Revolution in Britain, 1939-45", *The Frontline of Freedom: British Farming in the Second World War,* Eds Short, B., Watkins, C. and Martin, J., Exeter, British Agricultural History Society, 2007, pp.1-15.

26 DEFRA *The Women's Land Army, 2009* [online]. Available from: http://www.defra.gov.uk/farm/working/wla/. [Accessed 14th May 2009]

27 H.L. Smith, "The Womanpower Problem in Britain during the Second World War", *The Historical Journal*, 27, 4, 1984, pp.925-945, p.925.

28 S. Barber, "Irish Migrant Agricultural Labourers in Nineteenth Century Lincolnshire", Saothar: The Journal of Irish Labour History, 8, 1982, pp.10-23.

29 E.J.T. Collins, "Harvest Technology and Labour Supply in Britain, 1790-1870". *The Economic History Review, New Series*, Vol. 22, No. 3. (Dec 1969), pp.453-473.

30 E. Higgs, "Occupational Censuses and the Agricultural Workforce in Victorian England and Wales", *The Economic History Review*, New Series, Vol. 48, No. 4 (Nov 1995), pp.700-716.

31 S. Barber, op.cit. Also see Johnson, J.H. "Harvest Migration from Nineteenth century Ireland", *Transactions of the Institute of British Geographers,* No.41 (Jun 1967), pp.97-112.

32 J.H. Johnson, "Harvest Migration from Nineteenth Century Ireland", *Transactions of the Institute of British Geographers*, No.41 (Jun 1967), pp.97-112. Collins, E.J.T. op.cit.

33 E.J.T.Collins, *op. cit.*

34 Author Unknown, *Article MT130 Glimpses into the nineteenth century Broadside Ballad Trade* [online]. Available from www.mustrad.org.uk/articles/bbals_05htm. [Accessed 21st July 2010]

35 Lincolnshire County Council, *Nineteenth Century Miscellany*, date unknown [online]. Available from: http://www.lincolnshire.gov.uk/section.asp?catid=23034&docid=75965. [Accessed 26th July 2010].

36 E.J.T Collins, *op.cit.*

37 S. Barber, *op.cit.* p.18.

38 E.J.T Collins,. *op.cit.*

Chapter 5

MECHANISATION AND THE LINCOLNSHIRE MANUFACTURERS

Peter Dewey

.Introduction

The growth of the potato industry in Lincolnshire in the nineteenth and early twentieth centuries, coupled with the locating of so many agricultural machinery firms in the county, made it inevitable that a number of Lincolnshire manufacturers should move into the potato machinery business. We estimate that, from the beginnings of the British farm machinery industry in c.1850 until the present day, 109 British firms have been at some time engaged in making potato machinery. Seventeen of these were in Lincolnshire[1].

Before the First World War

Potato cultivation has its own requirements and problems, which have contributed to the slow advance of mechanisation in the industry. Usually planted in ridges, to ease drainage and keep the tubers from exposure to light (when they acquire a greenish tinge, unpopular with the consumer), they require much harrowing and weeding. Susceptible to disease, they also need spraying. At harvest, the top growth (haulms) can clog implements and machinery, and should be cut or killed off beforehand. In harvesting, potatoes are difficult to separate from clods of earth, sticky soil, and stones. They can be damaged easily by stones and hard clods, and by the harvesting machinery itself. All these considerations have affected the design and usage of implements and machinery[2].

The first stages of seed bed preparation did not require specialist equipment, the conventional plough and harrow sufficing to make a suitable tilth. The next stage was the use of the ridging plough, to create a furrow in which seed potatoes and dung could be placed. The plough was run between the furrows, its double mouldboard throwing the soil onto the furrows on either side, forming the ridges under which the crop would grow. Many plough-making firms produced ridging bodies for their ploughs. An example by John Cooke & Sons of Lincoln, from their 1876 catalogue, is shown as *Figure 5.1.* It was a design which had a long life, being almost identical to 'Cooke's Light Iron Ridging and Earthing Plough RDG', which was shown in their 1934 catalogue[3].

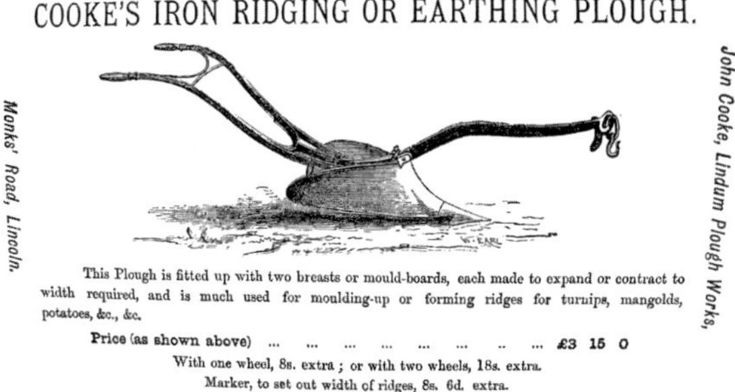

Figure 5.1
'Cooke's Iron Ridging or Earthing Plough', from the firm's catalogue of 1876.
(Museum of English Rural Life, TR SCM P2/B274)

Having sown the crop, harrowed and weeded it, and kept blight at bay, the problem arose of harvesting the potatoes, without damaging them unnecessarily. The first specialist implement developed for this was the 'digging plough'. This replaced the conventional plough mouldboard with a fan-shaped arrangement of iron bars, through which the earth fell back onto the ground, the potatoes being caught by the bars and pushed gently to one side, ready for the teams of hand pickers. Cooke produced such a plough, which was shown at the Royal Agricultural Society of England's (RASE) potato digger trials in 1887*(Figure 5.2).*

Another Lincolnshire firm in the business was J.B. Fenton of Sleaford, which flourished in the later nineteenth century. Although information on Fenton's pre-1914 ploughs is lacking, they may have been not dissimilar to those in their 1928 catalogue, when the firm offered: 'Fenton's New High-Head Potato Plough', as either a digger-cum-ridger, or separately as either digger or ridger *(Figure 5.3).*

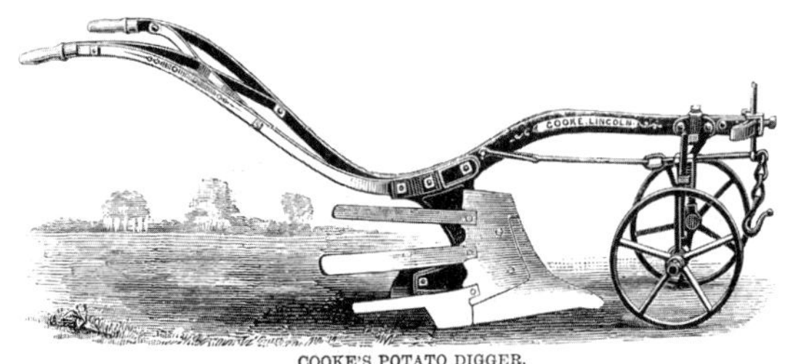

Figure 5.2
Cooke's Potato Digger (The Implement and Machinery Review, 1 November 1887, p.9997)

Competition for the Lincolnshire producers must have come from makers in nearby counties. The two largest plough producers in England before 1914 were almost certainly Howard of Bedford and Ransomes of Ipswich. Both produced potato digging ploughs similar to those of Cooke and Fenton, Howard's 1875 catalogue containing two types.[4]

The most important innovation in potato field machinery before 1914 was the 'spinner-digger', or 'spinner'. The first patent for this was taken out by Hanson in 1855, and his patent rights were shortly afterwards acquired by Coleman & Morton, of Chelmsford.[5] The spinner used a broad share at the front to loosen the potatoes

J. B. FENTON & SON, SLEAFORD. 11

When ordering Parts for L.W. Ploughs please state whether for No. 1 or No. 2.

THE BEST IN THE MARKET.

Fentons' New High-head Potato Plough No. 2
(SHOWN AS A DIGGER.) Weight, 2cwt.
Price, complete as a Digger and Ridger .. .. **£8 10s.**
As a Digger only, £7 5s. As a Ridger only, with Marker, £7 5s.
Beet Lifting Body to fit, **£2.**

A LIGHTER POTATO PLOUGH, No. 1.
As a Digger and Ridger, £7 10s. Ridger only, £6 5s. Digger only, £6 5s.
Front Raisers .. 16/- each. Back Raisers ... 9/ each.
ALL OUR PLOUGHS ARE TEMPLETED. Weight, 1cwt. 2qrs. 14lbs.

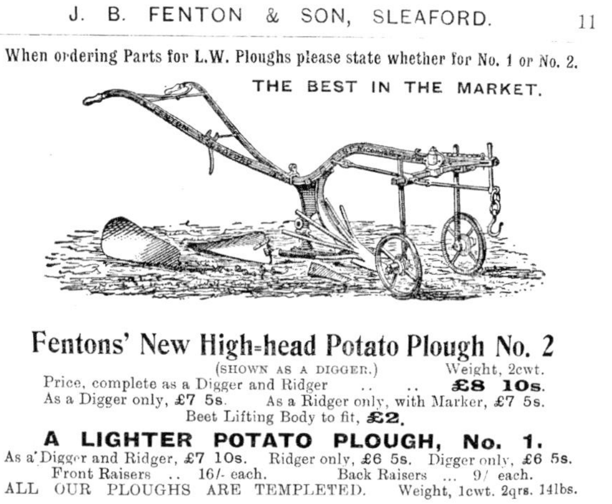

Figure 5.3
Fenton's new High-Head Potato Plough No. 2, from their 1928 catalogue. (Museum of English Rural Life, TR S4 P2B54)

from the ridge, and had a large wheel suspended transversely at the rear of the machine, being made to revolve by gearing driven from the land wheels. A series of fixed forks protruding from the rim of this wheel dug the potatoes out and flung them sideways, when they were caught by a net attached to an arm fixed to the side of the digger. They then fell in a row, and could be collected by hand.

The spinner was widely adopted, and came to dominate the potato harvest until after the Second World War. Many firms produced their own versions. One Lincoln firm that did so was Penney & Co., of Broadgate, Lincoln. Their machine *(Figure 5.4)* won a bronze medal at the 1878 Paris Exposition, and was advertised in *The Implement and Machinery Review* in 1879. A slightly modified version was shown at the RASE digger trials in 1887. The Penney digger was of particularly heavy construction, the firm explaining that it: '....was intended for the strong warp soils of Lincolnshire, where a heavy machine was indispensable.' In place of a net to catch the potatoes, it (and all but one of the other competitors in 1887) used a grille of iron bars, in spite of the greater degree of damage inherent in such a system.[6]

The spinner certainly saved labour, but it had disadvantages, due to the violence with which the forks engaged with the soil, flinging the potatoes inconveniently far, and perhaps severely damaging them. The eventual solution found for these problems

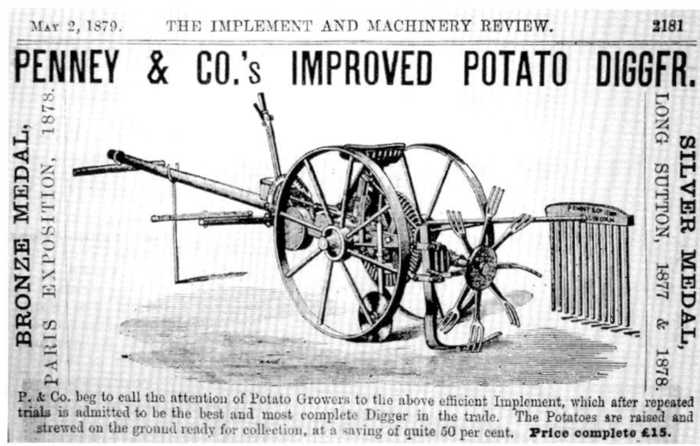

Figure 5.4
Advertisement for Penney & Co.'s Improved Potato Digger. (The Implement and Machinery Review, 2 May 1879, p. 2181)

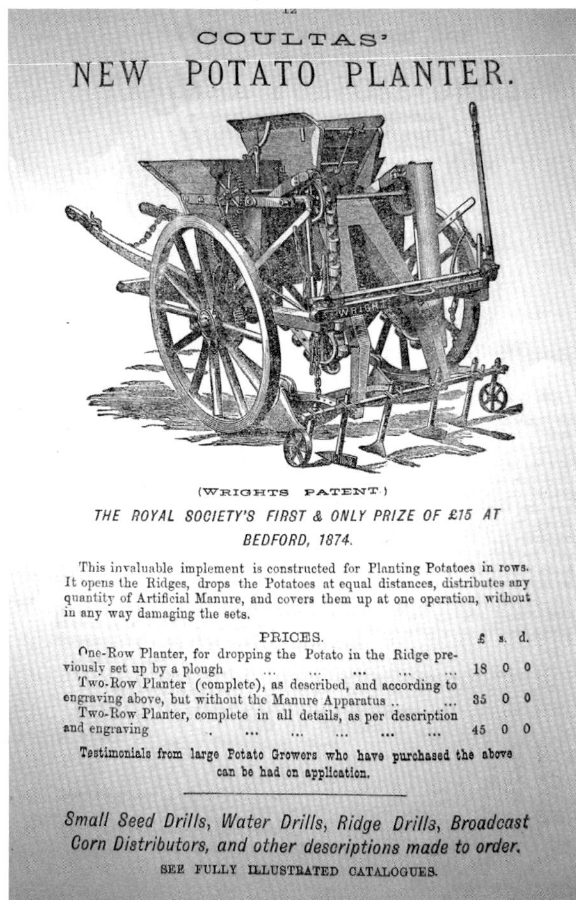

Figure 5.5
Coultas' New Potato Planter, from the firm's 1875 catalogue. *(Museum of English Rural Life)*

was to impart a feathering action to the forks, by means of an extra small wheel with a vertical linkage system, ensuring that the forks entered and left the ground vertically. This was much gentler on the tubers, causing them to be scattered with less force. At the RASE trials of potato diggers and sorters at Norwich in 1911, only machines with feathering action were considered eligible for awards. The first prize went to the Lincolnshire firm of Martin's Cultivator Company of Stamford, and the second to Blackstone, another Stamford firm already well known for its haymaking machinery. Serious competition was provided by Alexander Jack of Maybole (Ayr), Powell Bros. & Whitaker (Wrexham), who had both shown diggers in 1887, and by Ransomes of Ipswich. The judges remarked of the Martin machine: '.....with the aid of the peculiar feathering action the tubers were quietly dug, and well deposited ready for the pickers, very free from damage.' Another Lincolnshire firm which entered this market, although not until the next century, was J.B. Edlington of Gainsborough, which offered its 'Gainsboro' vertical-link tractor-drawn potato digger in 1933. It won the gold medal at the Holland (Lincs.) County Show in that year.[7]

By the 1870s, concern over the supply of manual labour focussed attention on the possibility of developing potato-planting machines. An early entrant into the market was the Lincolnshire firm of James Coultas of Grantham, whose main business was in seed drills.

Figure 5.6
Penney & Co., Potato Separator, 1874.
(Museum of English Rural Life, TR SCM P8B517)

Coultas' planter (using Wright's patent design) first appeared at the RASE Show at Hull in 1873, when it won a silver medal. At the Bedford meeting of the RASE in 1874 it won the first (and only) prize of £15, out of six machines entered (only three were tested). The firm was still producing its planter in 1896, when it was illustrated in the *Implement and Machinery Review*; it was a two-horse machine capable of planting ten acres a day.[8]

The third field in which mechanisation made progress before the First World War was in the sorting of potatoes. Penney & Co. was early in this market, with their separator of 1874, which sorted the potatoes into three sizes – small, seed, and marketable (more usually referred to as chats, seed and ware). It was said to be easily workable by a boy, and to process up to 240 stones (*a stone =14 lbs. = 6.35 kilos*) per hour.

As far as agricultural products went, Penney was probably better known for its rotary corn screens than its potato machines.[9] It is perhaps odd that they did not attempt to use the same rotary technology in their potato separators, which were of the flat-bed type. Rotary technology was the system employed by the probably rather larger firm of J.B. Edlington of Gainsborough, which (along with Cooch of Northampton) was one of the two largest firms competing at the 1911 RASE potato sorter trials. Out of five entrants, Cooch won the first prize. Both the Edlington and Cooch range of sorters were considerably extended over the years. In 1919, the Edlington 'Phoenix' sorter was to be offered in a power-driven version, and Cooch machines also came in powered versions. In 1949, Cooch would offer five models; two powered, two hand, and one which could be either.[10]

The final problem of harvesting, which was only part-solved before 1914, was the removal of haulm. This could be manually cut, harrowed, or reliance placed on the share of the spinner-digger to cut it – although digger shares could clog. A method growing in popularity was to spray it with sulphuric acid. Spraying for blight control was already established; the RASE held a trial of spraying machines at Cambridge in 1894. The prize was awarded to Strawsons of London. The local firm of Grattons (of Boston) was also in the sprayer market; it won the highest prize (silver) at the 1912 RASE Show,

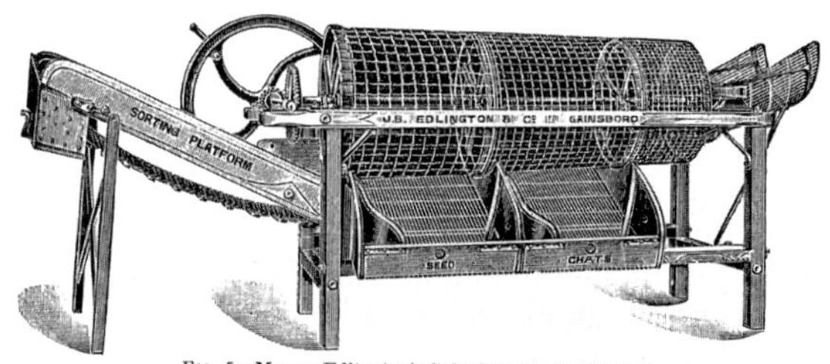

FIG. 5.—Messrs. Edlington's Cylindrical Potato Sorter.

Figure 5.7
Messrs. Edlington's Cylindrical Potato Sorter.
(Journal of the Royal Agricultural Society of England, 72 (1911), Figure 5, p.251)

for its dry powder sprayer, which was to be produced until the 1950s. The very large firm of Lincolnshire growers, Dennis and Sons, usually sprayed for blight beween two and five times in the season.[11]

After harvest, the potatoes were usually stored in the clamp, which was a circular or (more usually) long rectangle of ground in the field, excavated to the depth of a few inches. It was then piled with the potatoes, which were covered with a layer of straw, and then with soil, to insulate against frost. Later on in the autumn or early winter, the clamp would be opened and the potatoes sorted and bagged in the field, using machines such as those supplied by Edlington and Cooch. Clamp storage was predominant until after the Second World War, when indoor storage gained in popularity.

Seed potatoes can be planted before they sprout, but growers have for many years favoured pre-sprouting, or 'chitting' their seed. This shortens the growing time, allowing later planting, when the weather may be better, and produces a higher yield, which may be two tons per acre greater than that of unchitted seed. A disadvantage is that the sprouts are easily knocked off, and this made sowing by machine difficult.[12]

The production of suitable chitted seed requires certain conditions of controlled light and temperature, which are best provided indoors. The most favoured type of building for most of this period was in effect a large greenhouse. Lincolnshire growers were early in this movement. In the early twentieth century, three families were outstanding in the Lincolnshire potato business – Worth, Caudwell, and Dennis. *(See Chapter 3)* The Dennis family, known as 'the Potato Kings of Lincolnshire', were described by a U.S.A. observer in 1913 as: '....the pioneers in the most successful methods of storing their seed potatoes', having erected five large (160 x 24 feet) glass houses, each capable of storing 200 tons of seed potatoes. At harvest, the seed was sorted out from the wares and chats, put into crates or shallow boxes about three inches deep, and stacked in the open until threatened by frost, when the boxes would be moved into the chitting houses.[13]

A peculiarly Lincolnshire development was the on-farm narrow-gauge railway for moving potatoes *(See Chapter 5.1)*. In the low lying and soft soil of the Fens, harvesting and transporting potatoes in the autumn, often in wet conditions, led to ruination for farm roads. The solution to this was the on-farm light railway. After the First World War, large amounts of surplus track were on sale, and many farmers took the opportunity to install these as their own farm railway, which usually terminated at a hard-surfaced public road for onward carriage by lorry or cart. A few ran to main railway lines. Three ran to navigable waterways. Their wagons were usually horse-drawn, as the rails were not strong enough to take the weight of a locomotive. The high point was the late 1920s, with over 140 miles of line in at least fifty locations. Some of the very largest estates, heavily involved in potato-growing, built these lines around their farms. In 1920 Dennis's built the largest single network of all on their Nocton Estate (8,000 acres), laying down twenty-three miles of track.[14]

From the First World War to the 1950s

Technological change in this period took two forms. Specifically, there was one new machine, the elevator-digger. Generally, the industry began to adapt to the farm tractor.

The elevator-digger had at its front end a broad digging share, like a shovel. In action, as it was drawn along, the share scooped up the entire potato ridge, which was raised to the top of the machine on a moving elevator web, consisting of transverse steel bars linked together by continuous chain drives on either side of the machine. The soil (and hopefully the stones) fell back onto the ground through the gaps between the rods. The potatoes and most of the haulm continued to the top of the elevator, to be deposited on the ground in a narrow band, ready for hand picking.

The elevator-digger was pioneered in the U.S.A. at the end of the nineteenth century, although it does not seem to have been much in evidence in Britain before the First World War. In 1919, Leeds University trialled one (the Hoover, a U.S. make) against a Ransome's spinner-digger. The Hoover was found to save labour, requiring sixteen pickers, against the Ransome's twenty-one, but damaged a higher proportion of the crop (seven percent, as opposed to three per cent). Experience would also show that elevator chains wore rapidly.[15]

The elevator-digger was most useful on lighter soils, where it exposed more of the tubers than did the spinner. It worked faster and left the potatoes in a narrower band, but it was more prone to clogging and excessive wear. In very wet or heavy conditions the spinner would still be preferred. Later developments included: variable agitation of the web to eject the soil and stones without unnecessarily damaging the potatoes; an intermediate roller or web to eliminate the haulm before it reached the top of the elevator; two elevator webs, a primary 'digging' web to eliminate larger materials, and a secondary 'sieving' web to provide finer separation. By the 1950s, two-row elevator diggers were available, giving a faster work rate. On the larger models, a picking/bagging platform could be attached, to allow several people to travel with the machine and to separate

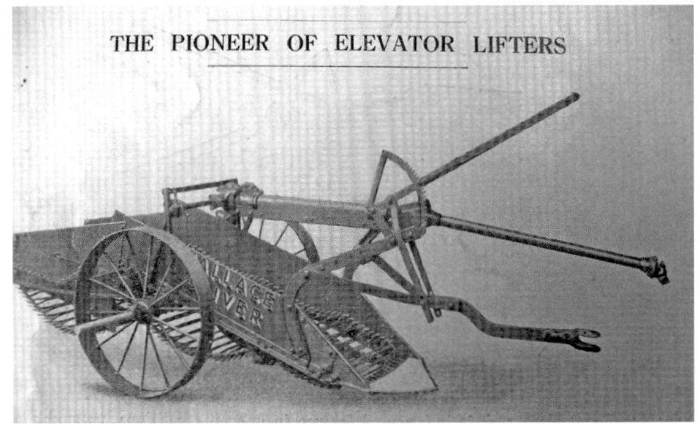

Figure 5.8
A British-marketed version of a U.S.A. elevator-digger: the Wallace 1949. John Wallace was a Glasgow firm. (Museum of English Rural Life TR AMD POB466)

Figure 5.9
An early British elevator-digger: the 'Angus' (L.O. Tractors), with power take-off drive (1949).
(Museum of English Rural Life TR AMD POB3472)

the potatoes manually from the haulm, stones and soil – a development prefiguring the later evolution of the 'complete harvester'.[16]

Early elevator-diggers were drawn by horses or (in the U.S.A.) mules, and the heavy work entailed in lifting the entire ridge required a team of at least two or three horses. By the 1930s, diggers driven from a tractor's power take-off (p.t.o.) were available, but British manufacturers did not enter the market until the 1940s. This may have been because they were already committed to the spinner, but also because the British tractor industry was in its infancy, and few tractors, except imported ones, had a p.t.o.[17] This changed after 1945, but until then most elevator-diggers were imported.

For the time being, British firms showed little interest in the elevator-digger. In 1932, Blackstone was still advertising its (horse-drawn) spinner-digger. In this, the digging forks rotated in a near-horizontal plane, but it was still a conventional spinner. The entry of Edlington into the digger market in 1933, when the firm produced a spinner-digger, has been mentioned above. Ransomes did not enter the elevator digger market until 1968, on taking over Johnson's Engineering.[18]

Rather than changing to the new elevator-diggers, firms adapted their extant machinery to the tractor. Until the development of hydraulic lifting systems on tractors, pioneered by Harry Ferguson in 1936, but not generally in use until after 1945, this was a matter of supplying their potato machinery with a tractor hitch. Ransome was to the fore in this process, a tractor-drawn version of its No.12 spinner-digger being available in 1920. In 1937 it would offer its No. 28A spinner-digger with 'optional headwheel and tractor attachment.' In 1935, Coultas offered its 'Patent combined three-row potato ridger and distributor', which was a fairly large machine, shown in the advertisement as being drawn by a tracked tractor. Also in 1935, Edlington offered their well-known 'Gainsboro' spinner digger as a two-horse machine, which: 'Can be fitted with Tractor Hitch in place of the above if required' *(Figure 5.10)*. Blackstone, which had merged its farm machinery business with Massey-Harris, and now traded as Massey-Harris-Blackstone, offered in the same year a self-lift (but not hydraulic) tractor version of its spinner-digger[19] *(Figure 5.11)*.

Nationally, potato growers relied overwhelmingly on the spinner and the horse to harvest the crop until after the Second World War. In May 1942, at the first national census of agricultural machinery in use on farms, there were recorded 24,852 spinners (21,565 horse-drawn), but only 2,549 elevator-diggers (2,051 horse-drawn) in England and Wales. Overall, elevator-diggers accounted for only 9.3 per cent of the combined total of spinners and elevators at work. It is likely that most of the elevator-diggers had been imported.[20]

By the late 1940s, the agricultural machinery industry had changed. Some notable firms had failed: Howard of Bedford in 1932, Cooke of Lincoln in 1938 (some of its business passing to Edlington). Fenton of Sleaford also disappeared, probably before 1939. But there were some new firms in the eastern counties: William Catchpole (Bury St. Edmunds); John Salmon (Dunmow), Johnsons Engineering (March, Cambs.), Root Harvesters (Peterborough), and Standen (Ely). These had all begun with machines for sugarbeet growing, which was subsidised by the government from 1926. Their move into potato machinery came after 1945.

Following the lead set by Harry Ferguson, other tractor firms developed their own hydraulic lifting systems.

Figure 5.10
Edlington's 'Gainsbro' Potato Digger, 1935.
(The Implement and Machinery Review, 1 July 1935)

In the late 1940s, Ransome undertook to make a range of implements for the Fordson tractor. Its 'New F-R *[Ford-Ransome]* Potato Digger' was recognisably a tractor-mounted version of the firm's pre-1914 spinner. Harry Ferguson, and after the merger with Massey-Harris in 1953, Massey-Harris-Ferguson (later Massey-Ferguson) also made a range of tractor-mounted potato machines.[21]

Other implements apart from diggers could be attached to the tractor. Several plough ridging bodies could be set on a toolbar, so that more than one row could be ridged. Ridge coverers (either a sort of small plough body, or a bobbin-shaped wheel) could also be supplied. The small plough type was one of the products of another Lincolnshire firm, Belton Bros & Drury of Eastoft, Scunthorpe, in 1953. 'Front Potato Coverers' of the bobbin sort were made by Leverton (Spalding) in 1955.[22]

The Massey-Harris-Blackstone Tractor Potato Digger fitted with Self-Lift.

Figure 5.11
Massey-Harris-Blackstone Tractor Potato Digger, fitted with self lift, 1935. (The Implement and Machinery Review, 1 August 1935)

By the late 1950s, a certain amount of progress had been made in potato planters, although even in 1965 a quarter of all potato seed was still being planted by hand.[23] Some machines were little more than tractor-towed platforms, upon which operators squatted uncomfortably, and dropped potatoes at intervals (usually prompted by the sound of a bell) into planting chutes. Some had become more sophisticated, semi-automatic, and capable of sowing chitted seed and fertiliser. The contrast between a simple planter and a more automated one is seen in the advertising leaflets for a Robot (Root Harvesters, 1959) and a Packman (1958) planter *(Figures 5.12 & 5.13)*.

The removal of haulm was a continuing problem. Haulm destruction by sulphuric acid continued to be practised, but, perhaps because of its corrosive effect on machinery, it was being supplanted by mechanical means. Gratton of Boston had produced a horse-drawn 'potato top cutter' in 1933.[24] By the late 1940s, several systems were being tried. Some had a rear-mounted revolving bar on the tractor, on which revolved chain flails driven by the tractor's power take-off. Other types depended on two horizontal cutting discs mounted on the front of the tractor (Bettinson produced this type in 1951), and yet another type had vertical discs mounted at the rear of the tractor.[25] By the early 1960s, the flail type had found favour. In 1963 the *Farm Implement and Machinery Review* featured three flail types: a Swiss-

Figure 5.12
Root Harvesters' 'Robot' 4-Row Potato Planter 1959.
(Museum of English Rural Life)

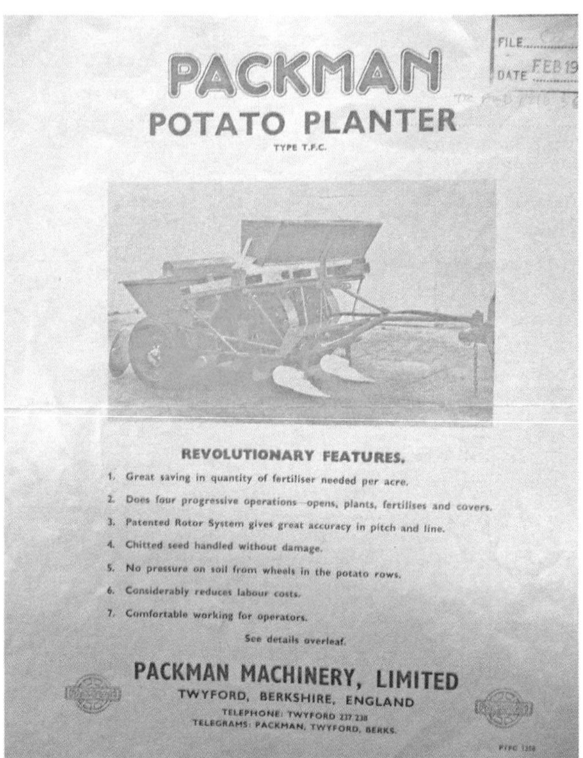

Figure 5.13
Packman T.F.C. Potato Planter 1958.
(Museum of English Rural Life)

designed four-row model made by Standen, soon to be in production; one already in production by Teagle (Truro, Cornwall); and an advertisement for a two-row topper by Johnson's Engineering.[26]

The continuing shrinkage of the rural labour force, both permanent and seasonal, was constantly focussing attention on ways to automate the harvesting of the potato crop. In the postwar period, this crystallised in the development of the 'complete harvester'. Satisfactory development took a very long time; the National Institute of Agricultural Engineering had been asked in 1949 by the Ministry of Agriculture to develop a prototype, but it was not until the early 1960s that satisfactory harvesters came on the market in quantity.[27]

The 'complete harvester' was in essence a development of the elevator-digger, on a larger scale, with more complex elevator systems and devices to get rid of clods, stones and haulm to the greatest possible extent, before the potatoes were elevated to an onboard manned sorting table, at which operatives could give a final sort by hand. The potatoes were then delivered by a side-elevator into a trailer being drawn alongside by a tractor, or bagged and dropped in the field. The advantages of this type of harvester were that it worked faster and saved labour – as well as allowing operatives to ride, rather than to walk (and stoop). A wide variety of configurations was adopted by the manufacturers. An early type was the 'Whitsed', by Root Harvesters, which was one of the models given a cash award by the judges at the first trial of complete harvesters held by the *RASE* in 1952.[28]

In this machine, the lifting of the crop was done by a broad share underneath, the ridge edges being sliced open by the large discs on either side. The potatoes travelled up the elevator web to the back of the machine and were then passed forwards on another web to a small sorting platform just behind the front wheels, at which the operative stood, before being delivered sideways. The operative(s) stood facing the sorting platform.

The rise of the complete harvester attracted new entrants to the industry. The successful machines at the 1952 RASE trials had been by Globe Harvester (London Colney), Root Harvesters (Peterborough), Johnson's (March, Cambs.), Packman (Twyford, Berks.), and a Swedish model, by Overum. At the eighth international harvester demonstration, in 1963, there were three Johnson models, a Massey-Ferguson, a Whitsed, a G.V.C., and three imported models. Import competition was to be an increasing feature of the harvester market.[29]

The road to full mechanisation

Larger harvesters and the adoption of hydraulic lifting systems on tractors had, by the 1960s, led to changes in post-harvest transporting and storing. Potatoes could now be discharged direct into a bulk trailer running alongside the harvester. Alternatively, the harvester (or the hand picker) could deliver the crop into pallet boxes, placed either on a trailer or on a tractor forklift. The crop was then delivered in bulk or box to an indoor store. The advantages of indoor storage included: less damage from fewer handling stages; more careful sorting; less risk of frost damage; easier access to the stored crop; and better working conditions. The potato clamp was going out of favour.[30]

The larger volumes to be handled led to changes in sorters and handling systems. Rotary sorters were abandoned in favour of flat-bed systems. Although still offering its rotary sorter in 1949, Edlington also offered a range of flat-bed sorters, either manual or powered. These got larger over time, and were accompanied

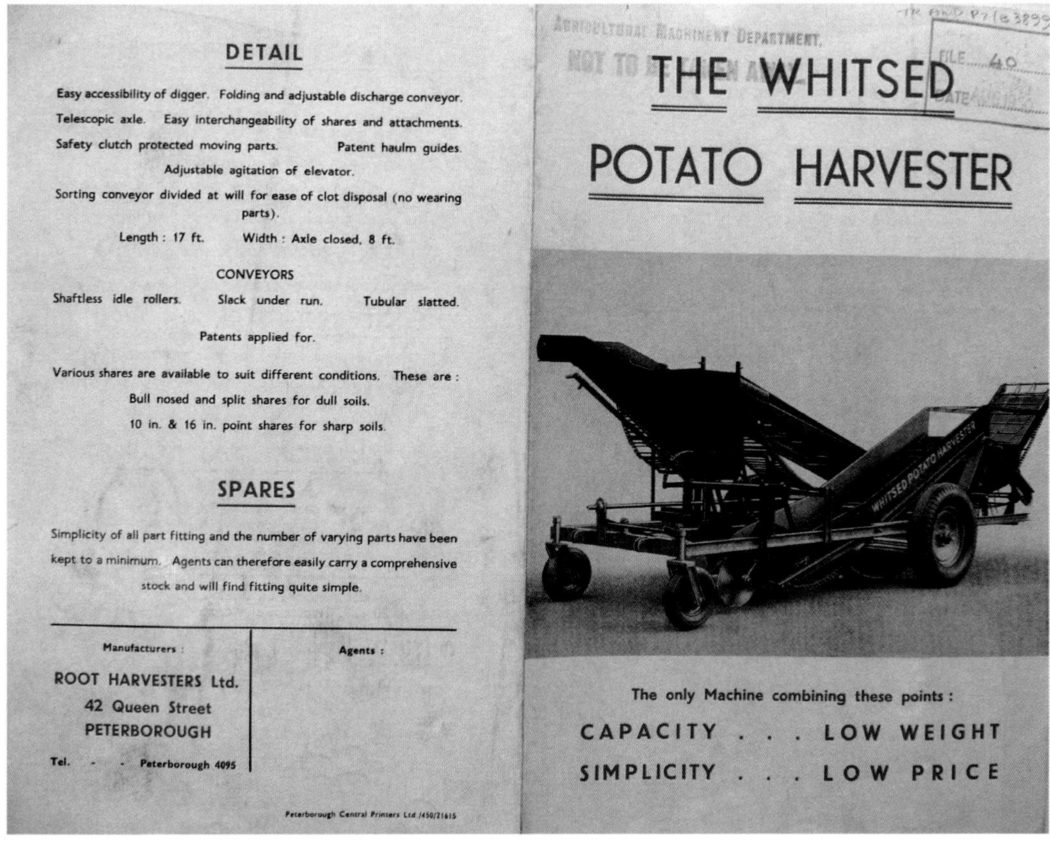

DETAIL

Easy accessibility of digger. Folding and adjustable discharge conveyor. Telescopic axle. Easy interchangeability of shares and attachments. Safety clutch protected moving parts. Patent haulm guides. Adjustable agitation of elevator. Sorting conveyor divided at will for ease of clot disposal (no wearing parts).

Length : 17 ft. Width : Axle closed, 8 ft.

CONVEYORS

Shaftless idle rollers. Slack under run. Tubular slatted.

Patents applied for.

Various shares are available to suit different conditions. These are :
Bull nosed and split shares for dull soils.
10 in. & 16 in. point shares for sharp soils.

SPARES

Simplicity of all part fitting and the number of varying parts have been kept to a minimum. Agents can therefore easily carry a comprehensive stock and will find fitting quite simple.

Manufacturers : ROOT HARVESTERS Ltd. 42 Queen Street PETERBOROUGH Tel. - - Peterborough 4095

Agents :

Peterborough Central Printers Ltd.

Figure 5.14
Root Harvesters Whitsed potato harvester 1950. (Museum of English Rural Life)

Figure 5.15
Standen Pearson 'Unistar' soil separator/destoner. *(Standen-Pearson)*

Figure 5.16
Reekie 'Cultistar' combined stone separator and cultivator. *(Reekie/Steve Thorley Potato Equipment)*

by the development of large hoppers and elevators. Edlington was one firm developing these products. Another Lincolnshire firm which became prominent in this field was Tong of Spilsby.[31]

By 1970 the complete harvester was harvesting 49% of the potato crop, the elevator digger 36%, and the spinner 15%.[32] But harvesting was some way off full mechanisation. In particular, the problem of damage by stones was yet unsolved, and cleaning them out of the crop still required hand pickers to ride on the 'complete' harvesters.

The last obstacle to full mechanisation – the removal of stones from the crop before harvesting - was achieved after the early 1970s, with the development of 'stone windrowing' machines, now usually referred to as 'stone separators'. The most advanced sequence of operation is now to plough and cultivate the soil, form raised seedbeds, and then pass a destoning machine along the beds. This lifts the beds, sifts out stones and clods by passing them up an elevating web conveyor, with power-driven agitators, and returns the soil to the ground. Some leave the soil in shaped ridges, ready for the planter. If not, a more traditional ridger is employed to give the beds final form. The stones are cross-elevated and deposited in a furrow at one side of the machine. They are subsequently pressed into the ground by the tractor wheels during planting, and this helps to drain

Figure 5.17
Standen Pearson trailed 2-row harvester T2. *(Standen-Pearson)*

Figure 5.18
Grimme 'Varitron' self-propelled harvester (with haulm topper in front). *(Grimme)*

Figure 5.19
Scott's 3-row haulm topper. (Scott's of Boston)

away the water which collects between the beds. After harvest the stones are collected up by the same destoning machine and replaced in the seedbed furrows.[33]

Stone separation has transformed the cultivation of potatoes, leading to much easier working of the soil, and minimal damage at harvesting. Harvesters now treat the crop much more gently, with the aid of softer web systems, using rubber or plastic rollers and multiple webs to separate the clods and stones from the potatoes, and to remove the haulm from the cut crop. The stream of material passing up the elevator is in any case much less mixed with stones than used to be the case, and this in turn minimises damage to the tubers.

There are two types of modern potato harvester. There are trailed harvesters, which are much larger versions of the elevator-digger. They are usually two-row machines, although three and four-row ones are available. There are also self-propelled harvesters, which are essentially combine harvesters for potatoes, with very large engines (300+ HP), perhaps running on tracks, and with the option of an onboard holding tank. Most types have eliminated the onboard operatives to sort the potatoes, and the only personnel employed are the drivers. Both trailed and self-propelled harvesters have become much larger, with a higher work-rate, using advanced hydraulics, electronic control systems, and depth sensing mechanisms.

A completely mechanised cultivation system at the beginning of the twenty-first century may comprise: plough; rotary power-tiller; soil separator; semi-mounted or trailed bedformer; semi-mounted or trailed planter; haulm topper; a trailed or self-propelled harvester. Some of these contemporary products are illustrated in *Figures 5.15 to 5.19.*

The changes in the international farm machinery industry in the last quarter of the twentieth century, combined with higher investment by manufacturers in more complex and expensive products, have led to a reduction in the number of firms. At present, the UK firms engaged in manufacturing field potato machinery are: Cousins of Emneth (Wisbech, Cambs.); CTM Root Crop Systems (Harpley, Norfolk); Reekie Potato Equipment (Boston, Lincs.)[34]; Scotts (Boston, Lincs.); Standen Pearson (Ely, Cambs.). Handling and sorting systems are manufactured by: David Harrison (Ely); Haith-Tickhill (Doncaster); R.J. Herbert (Marshland St. James, Cambs.); W.J. Morray (Braintree); Niagri (Lakenheath); Terry Johnson (Holbeach, Lincs.); Tong Peal (Spilsby, Lincs.).[35]

The British potato machinery industry faces much competition from imports. In 1996-9, UK manufacturers sold potato diggers and harvesters in the UK to the annual average value of £8.59 million. Average net imports were £3.42 million annually, making the average annual value of the total market £12.01 million. Imports thus accounted for 39.8% of the total market. Notable foreign competitors included Grimme (Germany), Gregoire-Besson (France), Agrifac (Holland), Underhaug (Holland) and Dewulf (Belgium).[36]

APPENDIX: LINCOLNSHIRE FIRMS MAKING POTATO MACHINERY

For this chapter, a list was made of all British manufacturers who made (or make) potato machinery, from the mid-nineteenth century onwards. This was compiled from manufacturers' publications (catalogues, brochures, price lists) held in the Museum of English Rural Life at the University of Reading, and at the Museum of Lincolnshire Life, containing information on: digger ploughs, planters, haulm cutters/pulverisers, spinner-diggers, elevator diggers, harvesters, and sorters. Ridgers were excluded, as not being necessarily dedicated to the potato business. I am indebted to Ken Redmore for further information on Lincolnshire firms. Additional information was taken from G.E. Fussell, *The Farmers Tools* (1952; repr.1981) and company websites. The result was a total of 109 firms. Of these, seventeen were/are located in Lincolnshire. They are:

Belton Bros. & Drury	Eastoft
P B Bettinson & Co. Ltd.	Holbeach
Blackstone & Co. Ltd.	Stamford
John Cooke & Sons	Lincoln
James Coultas Ltd.	Grantham
J. B. Edlington & Co. Ltd.	Gainsborough
J. B. Fenton	Sleaford
D. T. Gratton & Sons	Boston
P. & S.M. Johnson Ltd.	Holbeach
John W. Laming	Owston Ferry
H. Leverton & Co. Ltd.	Spalding
Martin Cultivator Company	Stamford
Penney & Co. Ltd.	Lincoln
Reekie Potato Equipment Ltd.	Boston
Shanks	Stamford
J. Shores & Co.	Owston Ferry
Tong Engineering Ltd.	Spilsby

All these were Lincolnshire manufacturers, with the possible exception of Shanks, which seems to have been a dealer on behalf of its parent manufacturer in Arbroath, Scotland.

Endnotes

1 See the Appendix to this chapter.

2 Ministry of Agriculture and Fisheries, Bulletin No. 94, *Potatoes* (4th ed., 1965), especially pp.31-7, 54-7.

3 Cooke's 1934 Catalogue, p.32, in Museum of Lincolnshire Life (hereafter MLL), Lincoln. There is an example of the RDG plough in the courtyard of this museum. See also H. Cooke, 'John Cooke of Lincoln', in *Ploughs, Chaff Cutters and Steam Engines: Lincolnshire's Agricultural Implement Makers,* edited by Ken Redmore, (Lincoln, 2007), p.33.

4 University of Reading, Museum of English Rural Life (hereafter MERL), *Catalogue of Agricultural Machinery issued by James and Frederick Howard, Britannia Iron Works, Bedford* MERL TR SCM P2/B409, pp.14-15.

5 J. Slight and R.S. Burn, *The Book of Farm Implements and Machines* (Edinburgh, 1858), p.203, Figure 283.

6 *The Implement and Machinery Review*, 1 November 1887, p.9996.

7 W.C. Brown, 'The Trials of Potato Diggers and Potato Sorters', *Journal of the Royal Agricultural Society of England* [hereafter *JRASE*], 72 (1911), pp.243-8; S. Edlington, T. Wall, and T.

Maidens, 'J.B. Edlington of Gainsborough: Agricultural Machine Makers', in Redmore, *Ploughs, Chaff Cutters and Steam Engines*, p.64; *The Implement and Machinery Review*, 1 December 1935, p.655.

8 'Report on the Trials of Implements at Bedford', *JRASE* 2nd series, 10 (1874), pp.661-2; C. Wilson, 'James Coultas of Grantham. Prize Drill Maker.', in Redmore, *Ploughs, Chaff Cutters and Steam Engines*, p.43.

9 MLL, Penney & Porter archive, 2BD 2/1/11, invoice heading of 30 March 1889.

10 W.C. Brown, 'The Trials of Potato Diggers and Potato Sorters, *JRASE* 72 (1919), pp.248-52; S. Edlington et al., 'J.B. Edlington' in Redmore, *Ploughs, Chaff Cutters and Steam Engines*, p.63; MERL, Cooch & Sons catalogue of June 1949.

11 C. Whitehead, 'The Trials of Spraying Machines at Cambridge', JRASE, 3rd. series, 5 (1894), pp.459-62; MLL, Gratton catalogue (1932); E.H. Grubb and W.S. Guilford, *The Potato: a compilation of information from every available source* (1913), p.468.

12 *Fream's Elements of Agriculture*, edited by D.H. Robinson (1949), p.220; J.A.S. Watson and J.A. More, *Agriculture: The Science and Practice of British Farming* (Edinburgh and London, 1945), p.256.

13 Grubb and Guilford, *The Potato*, pp.465-6.

14 S. Squires, *The Lincolnshire Potato Railways* (Usk, Mon., 2nd. ed., 2005), pp.21-5, 43, Appendix One.

15 J.R. Bond, *Farm Implements and Machinery* (1923), pp.164-5; C.H. Wendel, *Encyclopedia of American Farm Implements and Antiques* (Iola, Wisconsin, 2nd. ed., 2004), pp.352-9.

16 J.A.S. Watson and J.A. More, *Agriculture: the science and practice of British Farming* (11th ed., 1962), p.178.

17 The most widely employed British tractor, the Fordson, offered p.t.o. as an option in 1935, but it was only supplied as standard when the Fordson E27N came on the market in 1945.

18 MLL, Blackstone Potato Diggers Catalogue 1933 (publication no. 531); B. Bell, *Ransomes Sims & Jefferies, agricultural engineers: a history of their products* (Ipswich, 2001), pp.133-4.

19 *The Implement and Machinery Review*, 1 August 1935, p.367; 1 December 1935, p.655; 1 July 1935, p.294.; MERL, TR SIX P2/B141.

20 The National Archives, TNA BT 96/214, Appendix VI, *Return of Agricultural Machinery on 5th May 1942*.

21 B. Bell, *Ransomes Sims & Jefferies*, p.138; B. Bell, *Seventy Years of Farm Machinery. Part One: Seedtime* (Ipswich, 2009), p.99.

22 MLL, Belton Bros. & Drury Catalogue, 1 June 1953; MERL, Leverton catalogue (1955), TR AMD P2/B2749.

23 Ministry of Agriculture, *Potatoes*, p.32.

24 MLL, 'Gratton's Potato Top Cutter', leaflet of 1933; MERL, Bettinson leaflet TR AMD P2/B512 (October 1951).

25 D.H. Robinson, 'New ideas on growing potatoes', *JRASE,* 113 (1952), p.50.

26 *Farm Implement and Machinery Review* (1963), 1 June, p.848; 1 September, p.1260; 1 October, p.1398.

27 K. Grossfield and J.B. Heath, 'The Benefit and Cost of Government Support for Research and Development: A Case Study', *Economic Journal,* LXXVI (1966), p.538-9.

28 MERL, Root Harvesters catalogue, 1952, TR AMD P2/B3899; *JRASE* 113(1952), p.213.

29 Anon, 'Potato Harvesters Prove Their Worth: Heavy Land is Now No Problem', *Farm Implement and Machinery Review*, 1 November 1963, p.1507.

30 Potato Marketing Board, *Studies on the Relative Efficiency of Different Systems of Harvesting and Handling Potatoes into Store – 1965/66 & 1966/67*, Sutton Bridge Experimental Station Report No. 3 (1967), p.2; Robinson, 'New Ideas on Growing Potatoes', p.5; Watson and More, Agriculture (1945), p.270.

31 MLL, Edlington catalogues of 1959 and c.1975; Tong catalogues 1950, 1956, 1988; S.Edlington et al., 'J.B.Edlington', p.65.

32 Potato Marketing Board, *The Utilization and Performance of Potato Harvesters 1971,* Farm Mechanisation Studies No. 24 (Cowley, 1972), p.3.

33 B. Bell, *Farm Machinery* (Ipswich, 5th ed., 2005), p.248.

34 The rights to the Reekie brand of potato machinery, which had originated in Scotland, were acquired by Steve Thorley Potato Equipment, of Algarkirk, Boston, Lincs. in 2005.

35 Information from *www.agmachine.com* and individual company websites.

36 Office of National Statistics, *PRA 52 Product Sales and Trade 1999, Tractors, agricultural and forestry machinery*, (1999) p.59.

5.1 POTATO RAILWAYS

Stewart Squires

Several references are made throughout this book to the use of light narrow gauge railways on Lincolnshire farms. Their history is described in detail in the book *Lincolnshire Potato Railways*[1] but they are part of the story of the potato in the county so this brief summary is included here.

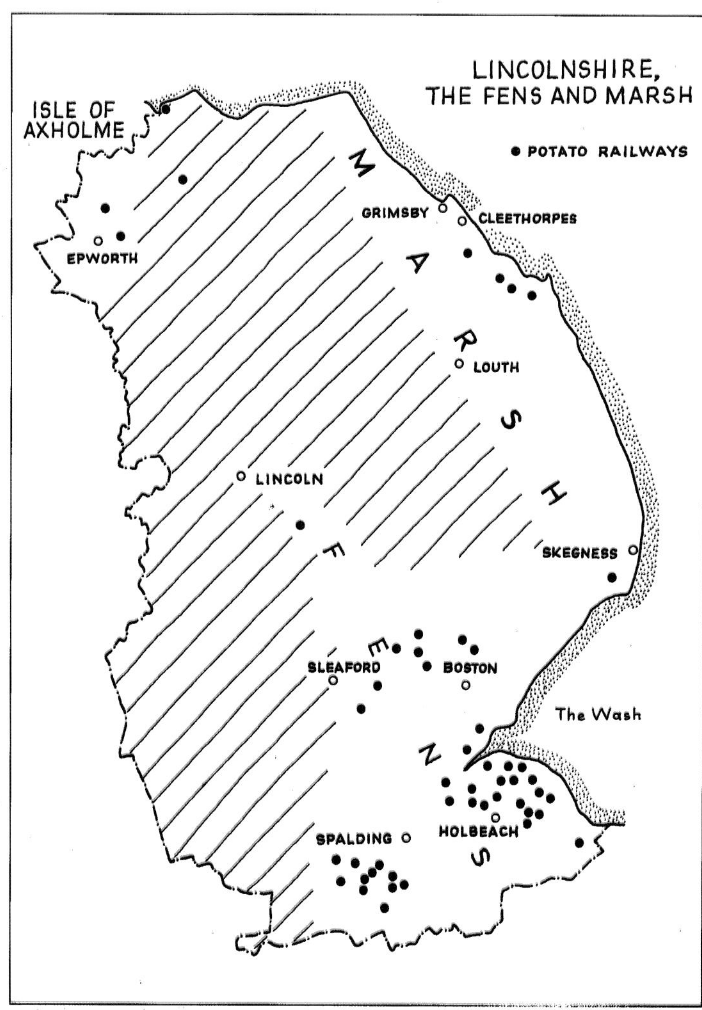

Figure 5.1.1
The locations of the Lincolnshire farms which used a narrow gauge railway. (Source: Lincolnshire Potato Railways)

The history of the use of rails on farms is as old as the history of railways themselves. An early record appeared in *The Times* in 1850, with the report of a tramway in Lancashire used to take the turnip crop off heavy land, very economic to lay and move around the farm as needed. In the 1850s the growing of turnips was a much greater industry than the growing of potatoes but the problems the farmers had of getting heavy crops on and off their land was the same.

In Lincolnshire the most widespread use of narrow gauge railways was on farms, with over 140 route miles of track laid on farms in at least fifty separate locations, almost all on the lower lying lands of the Fens and Marsh *(Figure 5.1.1)*. The shape of many farms suited the use of a railway. On the more recently reclaimed fenlands farms tended to be of long rectangular blocks, their boundaries defined by drainage dykes. A railway down the centre served the whole farm. On larger farms the rails often spread out from the centre like the spokes of a wheel.

The farm railways usually terminated at a hard surfaced public road for onward carriage by cart or lorry. Seven linked with a railway station or goods yard on the national railway network while three led to a navigable river.

Horses were the usual motive power but some potato railways, notably the greatest in extent, the Nocton Estate and Worth's Fleet Light Railway, used locomotives as well. Most were petrol or diesel engined but the Dennis estates at both Nocton and at Deeping St Nicholas used steam, the former for a short lived period. At least one farmer made his own locomotive.

Figure 5.1.2
The railway laid on George Caudwell's Wraggmarsh House Farm at Weston, near Spalding. Peas being taken for vining form the load here, illustrating how that once laid for potatoes they were used for other crops as well. The modernization of this farm railway in 1931 included the introduction of at least one diesel-engined Hudson locomotive.
(Stewart Squires, via George Hay)

Farm railways were not confined to Lincolnshire and they were also found in south Yorkshire and Cambridgeshire, again on fenland soils and often just outside the Lincolnshire County boundary. Their use in other counties was not as widespread and was often on a farm owned by a Lincolnshire based farmer. One example was at Red House Farm, Hatfield Chase, Yorkshire, owned by John Henry Bletcher of Belton who had a light railway to link his North Moor Farm and Old Farm in the Isle of Axholme with Hagg Lane Siding on the Axholme Joint Railway. He was also Chairman of the Axholme Joint Railway. Another example is the light railway at Mettleham Farm, Soham, near Ely, owned by AH Worth of Fleet *(see Chapter 3)*.

The history of farm railways begins in France. In the late nineteenth century Paul Decauville inherited an agricultural machinery business and devised a system of 60cm gauge portable light railway for use on farms. Easily transportable, this was designed to be laid by local labour without the need to use any specialised equipment. As Chapter 3 shows, George Caudwell was the first to use one in Lincolnshire in 1908, *(Figure 5.1.2)* closely followed by AH Worth in 1909. But at first a railway was a major capital outlay and it took the aftermath of World War I to make a railway affordable for many Lincolnshire farmers. After the end of the War large amounts of track, wagons and other equipment used to serve the needs of the British Army was sold cheaply as surplus to requirements and the Lincolnshire farm railways were able to reach their zenith.

The high point was the late 1920s when 35 farm railways were in operation in the County. The first loss came in the late 1920s, followed by two others in the 1930s. On the outbreak of World War II, however, most were still in operation. From this time tractors increasingly began to replace horses and many miles of concrete farm roads were constructed. In 1945, the railways were being used at least at 24 locations. By the end of 1950 only five remained. In 1955 only that at Nocton remained to soldier on for a few years longer *(Figure 5.1.3)*. Most of this was to be closed in 1960, although one last vestige remained in use until 1969.

This has led to an unusual present day feature that the Lincolnshire landscape has in common with the landscapes of parts of the former front lines on the Western Front in France and Belgium. Many farms have fence posts formed from cut lengths of old rail, an example of recycling practised by the farming community for many years.

Figure 5.1.3
Wasps Nest near Nocton, in 1937. Motor Rail locomotive, No 5 hauling a load of bagged potatoes from the fen to the railhead adjacent to Nocton and Dunston station.
(Museum of English Rural Life)

No farm railways now survive in Lincolnshire. However, all was not lost as track, engines and rolling stock from one of them, at Nocton, survived to create a new line, the Lincolnshire Coast Light Railway, albeit in a new guise, that of a passenger carrying narrow gauge railway, at Winthorpe, near Skegness. The North Ings Farm railway, at Dorrington north of Sleaford, is another which keeps the memory alive with regular open days throughout the summer.

Endnote

1 Stewart E Squires, *The Lincolnshire Potato Railways*, Second revised edition, (Usk 2005).

Chapter 6

FISH AND CHIPS

Stewart Squires

In the Spring of 2010 Britain celebrated 150 years of fish and chips.[1] The true origins of this staple food of the British diet are obscured by the mists of time. What this essay attempts to do is to identify a major role for Lincolnshire potatoes and Grimsby fish in the development of the dish, and to chart the growth of the trade and its maintenance over that period.

Fried fish and fried potatoes were foods that were originally sold separately. Neither is British in origin but it was in Britain that the two were put together to create what many regard as our national dish.

Battered fried fish is believed to be been introduced into London from the end of the sixteenth century with the arrival of Jewish Refugees from Portugal and Spain, escaping from the Inquisition. Jews from Portugal in particular ate fried fish and by the 1830s it became an important food for poor people in the capital. It was tasty, cheap and filling and was eaten both hot and cold. In *Oliver Twist,* first published in 1838, Charles Dickens described the squalid conditions in which many of the citizens lived their lives and referred to a 'fried fish warehouse.' In 1846 a Jewish cookery book, published in London, included a recipe for fried fish.

The deep frying of fish disguised its poor quality, both the cheaper types used and its state of freshness, and this may be a reason for it becoming a staple of the poor.

Chips are said to have originated in both Belgium and France. A Belgian housewife is said to have fried potatoes in place of fish in 1680 when the River Meuse was frozen and fish was not available. In 1854 a cookery book written by French Chef Alexis Soyer included a recipe for fried cooked potatoes. It may be that deep frying was not successful until cheaper cooking fats, such as cottonseed oil, became available in the 1860s.[2]

It was in the middle of the nineteenth century that fish and chips first came together to be sold. John Lees started selling fish and chips at Tommyfield Market in Oldham in 1858. Starting in a wooden hut, he later opened a shop nearby. Today a blue plaque marks the site *(Figure 6.1).* In 1860 or 1863 Joseph Malin opened a similar shop in Cleveland Street in the East End of London.

By 1900 such was the popularity of fish and chips that there were more than 30,000 shops nationwide.[3] The first Fish Restaurant was the initiative of Samuel Isaacs who ran a thriving wholesale and retail fish business throughout London and the South of England in the latter part of the nineteenth century. His first restaurant opened in London in 1896 serving fish and chips, bread and butter and tea for nine pence; its popularity ensured a rapid expansion of the chain through the working-class areas of London as well as into Clacton, Brighton, Ramsgate and Margate, the seaside towns to which those people went on holiday.

So, in 1858 fish and chips are first sold together as a take-away dish in Oldham. What is the link between Oldham and Lincolnshire? There were three things that needed to come together to feed the growth of fish and chip shops. These are: fish and potatoes in the right quantities and at the right price; a market for them; and the means of transporting those quantities of the fresh food from the supplier to the shop. Step forward the County of Lincolnshire and

Figure 6.1 The Blue Plaque in Oldham marking the site of the first Fish and Chip shop. *(Courtesy of Oldham Metropolitan Borough Council)*

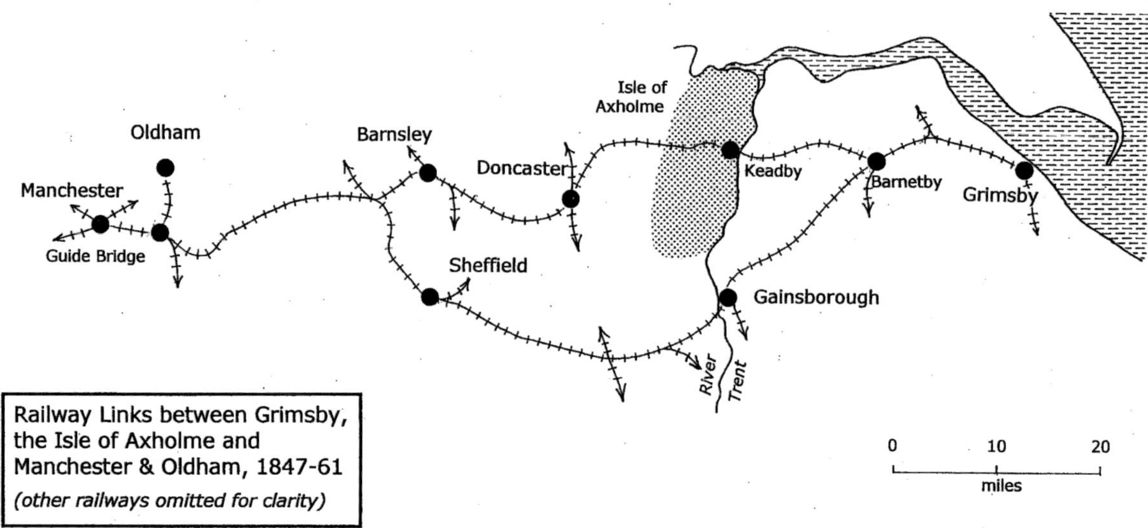

Figure 6.2
Railway links between Grimsby, the Isle of Axholme and Manchester and Oldham, 1847-61.
(Map drawn by Ken Redmore)

the Manchester, Sheffield and Lincolnshire Railway (MSLR). Lincolnshire was connected to Manchester by rail at that time. Manchester was the principal city at the west end of the MSLR linked with the Isle of Axholme, which was growing potatoes in large quantities, and with Grimsby, which was rapidly growing as a fishing port *(Figure 6.2).*

The growing of potatoes was well established in Lincolnshire by the late eighteenth century.[4] Many farmers in the Fens and the Isle of Axholme grew a few acres and from the 1830s the potato became the major crop in the Isle of Axholme. The larger farmers here brought manure from Hull, Leeds and Sheffield to provide the right soil conditions. In 1856 it was recorded that large quantities of flax and hemp, as well as corn, rape and turnips were being produced in the Isle, 'as also potatoes in large quantities.' [5] This is the only reference to potatoes being grown on a large scale in that source at that time.

By 1872 the culture of potatoes in the Isle of Axholme was said to be very extensive, comprising nearly one third of the crop of the improved farmland annually.[6] At that time 'some potatoes' were being grown in the Lincolnshire Fens but 'many potatoes' in the Marsh and between Wainfleet and Boston 'the quantity of potatoes now grown is astonishing.'

Why were potatoes being grown in such quantities in the Isle of Axholme? The answer is the influence of water transport. The Isle had very good transport links, via the rivers Humber, Trent and Ouse and their connecting canals and navigations, with Hull, Sheffield, Rotherham, Doncaster, Huddersfield, Wakefield, Leeds and York. All these towns and cities had expanding populations of people who had to be fed. The population of Leeds, for example, trebled in the fifty years between 1801 and 1851. The import of manure from Hull, Leeds and Sheffield has already been referred to above and this, too, could be brought in by boat. So, the ideal conditions for the development of potato growing in the County were met in that there was a product, a market and a means of linking the two.

The MSLR was created in 1847. It was an amalgamation of four railway companies who were involved in creating parts of a link between Manchester, Ashton-under-Lyne, Stalybridge, Barnsley and Sheffield, and Grimsby. At the time of its creation lines ran only from Manchester, Sheffield and Barnsley. By 1850 the link from Sheffield via Gainsborough to Grimsby was complete and a major east/west route across northern Britain was in operation.[7] In 1858 the South Yorkshire Railway and River Dun (sic) Navigation linked Barnsley with Keadby, a route subsequently extended to Barnetby in 1866. In 1864 the South Yorkshire Railway was leased to the MSLR.[8] Oldham was first linked by railway with Manchester by the Lancashire and Yorkshire Railway in 1847. The Oldham, Ashton-under-Lyne and Guide Bridge Junction Railway opened in 1861. Promoted by the MSLR, it was leased jointly to them and the London and North Western Railway but absorbed into the MSLR from1862.

The foregoing does not set out to describe the creating of all of the railways and lines that became part of the MSLR. What it does is to show that the Isle of Axholme, through Gainsborough from 1850 and Keadby from 1858, was linked by the MSLR with South Yorkshire and with the Manchester conurbation. That link extended to Oldham from 1861.

The Grimsby Haven Company opened their dock in Grimsby in 1800. In 1845 they became the Grimsby Docks Company and soon merged with the MSLR. The railway company revitalised the port with their Royal Dock, built 1845-52.[9] In 1854 a six acre fish dock, adjacent to the Royal Dock, opened and the foundation laid for what was to become the greatest fishing port in the world *(Figure 6.3).*

The creation of the fishing industry was an initiative by the MSLR. They built the fish dock and, together with the Great Northern and Midland Railways, they sponsored the formation of the Deep Sea Fishing Company, launched with nine vessels. To further encourage the industry, they quoted low rates for transport. Following completion of the dock they built an ice house and also, with the Great Northern Railway, built fifty houses for fishermen. In 1852 500 tons of fish were forwarded by rail from Grimsby. By 1863 this had risen to 10,360 tons with some 300 fishing smacks operating from the dock.[10]

The MSLR was a very active company, developing its links between east and west, and promoting business between them. The chairman of the railway from 1847 to 1860 was the second Earl of Yarborough. He lived at Brocklesby Hall in North Lincolnshire and was also the chairman of the Grimsby Docks Company.

The development of Grimsby as a fishing port continued. Fish Dock No. 2 opened in 1886 with Fish Dock No. 3 in 1934. 45,000 tons of fish were landed in 1880, rising to 70,000 in 1890 when about 800 trawlers were operating from the port. By 1900 the tonnage had risen to 135,000, increasing again to 175,000 in 1909.[11] In 1920 the tonnage peaked at about 220,316 with the period between 1911 and the end of the 1920s averaging around 170,000 tons per annum.[12]

Prior to the First World War over 90% of the fish was despatched by rail. In 1928 normally five main line fish trains departed every day, with additional consignments on thirteen passenger trains and four goods trains *(Figure 6.4).* What made Grimsby fish so distinctive was its distribution around the British Isles and beyond. Consignments were despatched to over 3000 stations in England and Wales and also to Scotland, Ireland, the Channel Islands, the Isle of Man and France. Dried fish was exported worldwide, principally to Spain, Portugal Argentina, Chile, Peru and Ecuador.[13]

The busiest time of year was the week before Easter at a time when religious observance was widespread and demanded that fish be eaten on Good Friday. In 1928 the Wednesday before Good Friday saw 1348 tons of fish despatched in 346 van loads.[14] In 1931 263 vessels discharged in Easter Week and 3442 tons of fish were

Figure 6.3
Unloading fish at Henderson Jetty, Fish Dock No 2, Grimsby, c1926. (LNER Magazine, now published in digital format by the Great Eastern Railway Society)

Figure 6.4
The London and North Eastern Railway (LNER) carried fish from several ports in the north and east of Britain, loading between 3500 and 4000 wagons every week, two thirds from Hull and Grimsby. In 1928 they carried fish mainly in specially built ventilated vans. Of the three shown here that at the top was their standard fish van in general use. The two larger wagon types were provided specially for the traffic from Grimsby. *(LNER Magazine, now published in digital format by the Great Eastern Railway Society)*

despatched by rail in four days.[15] In 1937 for the same week 15,000 tons of fish were landed with 10,000 tons going by rail.[16] It is for this reason that Grimsby was known as the greatest fishing port in the world.

By 1957 eight express trains were leaving Grimsby every day: for Banbury, Leicester, Leeds, Manchester and Nottingham and three to London. From the early 1960s almost all this traffic was transferred to road haulage.[17]

In 1980 there were 238 vessels based here, landing 66,000 tons of fish annually.[18] This was after the 1972 Cod War with Iceland and the start of the rundown of the British fishing industry. Grimsby's link with the fish industry remains, however, to this day. It still has the largest fish market in the UK but with fish landed from Icelandic ships or brought in by road. The town is also home to around 500 food related companies and it is one of the largest concentrations of food manufacture, research, storage and distribution in Europe.

Figure 6.5
Fishing boats coaling from lighters in Grimsby Fish Docks, 1928. *(LNER Magazine, now published in digital format by the Great Eastern Railway Society)*

Figure 6.6
The Kings Cross Potato Market, established by the Great Northern Railway, seen here in 1864.
(LNER Magazine, now published in digital format by the Great Eastern Railway Society)

Before leaving the town it should be noted that up to the middle of the nineteenth century almost all fishing boats relied on steam power for their propulsion and this, together with the export of coal through the commercial dock, generated a substantial coal traffic to Grimsby. In the mid 1920s around 900,000 tons of coal per year were consumed by the town's steam trawlers, giving rise to the maxim that it took 5 tons of coal to catch 1 ton of fish[19] *(Figure 6.5).*

So the development and success of Grimsby and its fishing industry was directly attributable to the railways. They were also responsible for the development of the potato industry in the County and we have seen something of the role of the MSLR above. The Great Northern Railway (GNR) also played its part. The very first length of line on which their trains ran was that between Grimsby and Boston in 1848. Later the same year trains were running on to Peterborough, via Boston, and from Boston to Lincoln. The link from Peterborough to London Kings Cross was completed in

Figure 6.7
At Kings Cross Potato Market in 1929, sacks of potatoes, after being unloaded from railway wagons, are sorted and repacked for retailers. *(LNER Magazine, now published in digital format by the Great Eastern Railway Society)*

Figure 6.8
Kings Cross Potato Market in 1929.
Potatoes are being sorted from sacks into boxes. These are for export by ship. *(LNER Magazine, now published in digital format by the Great Eastern Railway Society)*

1852. Right from these early days the GNR provided a potato market alongside Kings Cross, *(Figures 6.6, 6.7 and 6.8))* initially to deal solely with Lincolnshire potatoes but later with all of the potatoes they brought to the City.[20]

The GNR recognised that even with many village stations on the railways around the Boston and Spalding area many farms were still a long way from them. The distances of cartage from farm to station could be significant, especially for a bulky crop like potatoes.

The GNR made generous allowances to farmers to cover the cost of cartage which, in turn, encouraged the provision of the carting services. The GNR also tackled the organisation and centralisation of the traffic with very low rates for consignment in bulk and special rates for smaller quantities of four and five tons.

The loaded wagons were picked up at the wayside stations by the local goods trains and taken to Boston and Spalding (*Figures 6.9, 6.10 and 6.11*). During the First World War, for six months of the year, two to four hundred wagon loads of potatoes were despatched from south Lincolnshire every day.[21] Traffic from Spalding went to London and also the south and the southwest. From Boston trains ran for the Newcastle area, the West Riding of Yorkshire, Liverpool and Manchester. Trains also ran to the docks in London, Liverpool and Hull for export. By 1931 the station yard in Spalding was provided with a potato dock dedicated to that traffic and in that year despatched 12,000 tons.[22]

William Dennis, potato merchant and grower, known as the Potato King, built his business up to the extent that it had its own large rail-served warehouse in the station yard at Kirton, south of Boston. In 1904 the company despatched 1993 wagonloads from Kirton Station, to 250 places in Britain.[23] *(See Chapter 3)*

Once lifted out of the ground potatoes would be stored in clamps. These were built in the fields at a point where they would be accessible throughout the winter. Potatoes were taken from the clamps, riddled, that is sorted for size, and bagged up for sale and onward transhipment.

Writing in his book published in 1914, *Highways and Byways of Lincolnshire*, W. F. Rawnsley, in his visit to the Spalding area, said:

> From Deeping to Spalding the road is a typical fen road, three little inns and a few farm cottages and the occasional line of white smoke on the perfectly straight Peterborough to Boston railway is all there is to see save the crops or the long potato graves which are mostly by the roadside.
>
> The potato trade is a very large one. Every cart or wagon we passed at Easter time on the roads between Deeping and Kirton in Holland was loaded with sacks of potatoes, and all the farm hands were busy uncovering the pits and sorting the tubers. Donington and Kirton seem to be the centre of the trade, Kirton being the home of the man who is known as the potato king, and has many thousands of acres of fenland for this crop alone.

In the 1930s one farm at Fleet, east of Spalding, despatched 17,000 tons of produce annually, 10,000 of which were potatoes. Large amounts in the form of seed potatoes and fertilisers also had to be imported.

Almost routinely, when railways were promoted companies claimed that agriculture would benefit. Again routinely, farmers accessed the railway service through the sidings that were provided at the village stations. It was not common to provide stations that were for goods only, let alone provide an individual farmer with a siding such as a lineside factory might have. In Lincolnshire this approach began to change in the late nineteenth century, albeit by that time most of the county network had been established.

In 1882 the final link in what became the Great Northern and Great Eastern Joint Railway (GN&GEJR) was forged when the line between Lincoln and Spalding via Sleaford opened. This linked northwards from Lincoln to Gainsborough with an earlier route, substantially rebuilt at this time. Here for the first time, between Spalding and Gainsborough, no less than nine separate sidings were provided, away from the village stations, for goods traffic only, principally handling coal and agricultural produce.[24]

The passing of the Light Railways Act in 1896 spawned the Axholme Joint Railway, opened in stages from 1900 to 1909, its trains running between Goole and Haxey Junction, passing through Crowle, Belton, Epworth and Haxey, with branches to Fockerby and Hatfield Moor, the latter for goods only. The thirty miles of railway had nine stations for passengers and goods but what made it unusual and unique in Lincolnshire was no fewer than seventeen additional goods depots meeting the agricultural needs of the Isle of Axholme, most serving one individual farm. The potatoes, peas and carrots grown here now had almost direct access between field and market.[25]

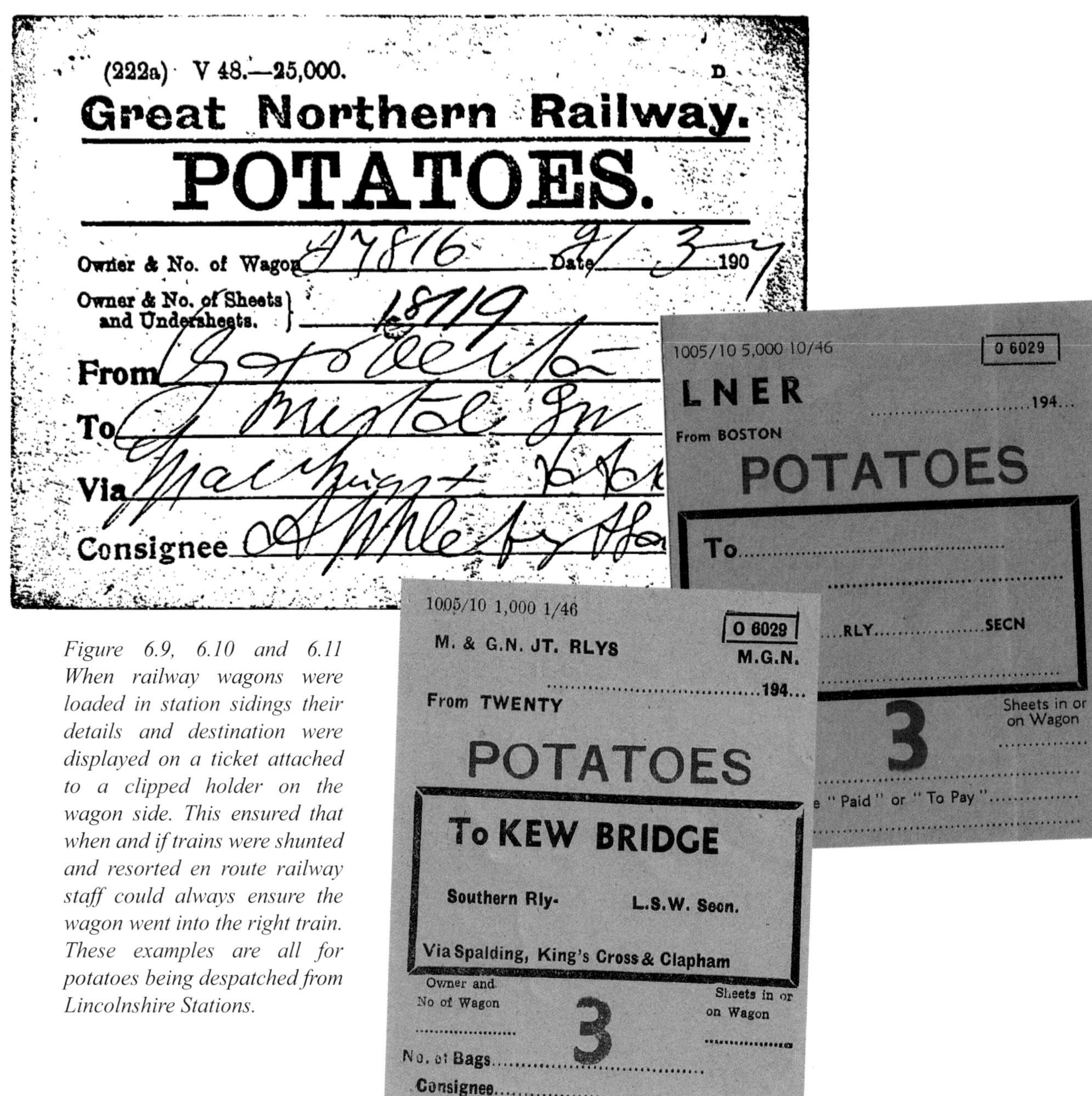

(222a) V 48.—25,000. D

Great Northern Railway.

POTATOES.

Owner & No. of Wagon ... Date ... 190

Owner & No. of Sheets and Undersheets.

From

To

Via

Consignee

1005/10 5,000 10/46 | 0 6029

LNER ....194...

From BOSTON

POTATOES

To....

RLY.... SECN

3

Sheets in or on Wagon

"Paid" or "To Pay"....

1005/10 1,000 1/46 | 0 6029

M. & G.N. JT. RLYS | M.G.N.

....194...

From TWENTY

POTATOES

To KEW BRIDGE

Southern Rly- L.S.W. Secn.

Via Spalding, King's Cross & Clapham

Owner and No of Wagon

3

Sheets in or on Wagon

No. of Bags....

Consignee....

Figure 6.9, 6.10 and 6.11 When railway wagons were loaded in station sidings their details and destination were displayed on a ticket attached to a clipped holder on the wagon side. This ensured that when and if trains were shunted and resorted en route railway staff could always ensure the wagon went into the right train. These examples are all for potatoes being despatched from Lincolnshire Stations.

Figure 6.9 is a copy of a label issued by the Great Northern Railway in 1907 for a wagon taking potatoes from Gosberton to Bristol on the Great Western Railway, travelling via March, Kings Cross (always Kings X in railway shorthand) and Acton. Figures 6.10 and 6.11 are unused labels of the 1940s. The former is for potatoes from Boston on the London and North Eastern Railway (LNER) and the latter for a wagon from Twenty station, east of Bourne on the Midland and Great Northern Joint Railway (M&GN), to Kew Bridge on the Southern Railway, via Spalding, Kings Cross and Clapham. *(Figures 6.9 and 6.11 from Stewart Squires collection; Figure 6.10 courtesy of Ken Hollamby)*

The links between Lincolnshire fish and potatoes on the one hand and the fish and chip shops and restaurants nationwide on the other, over the last 150 years, has been crucial. Fish and potatoes are still among the county's products today and continue to provide for the national need. Even today there are around 8100 fish and chip shops across the UK, eight for every one McDonalds outlet.[26]

Not for nothing did a fish and chip shop I remember in Blackpool in 1970 proclaim on a board outside in the street 'Frying tonight, new Lincolnshire Pot's' as a mark of the quality it was proud to provide.

Endnotes

1 For example; *The history of fish and chips*, Woman's Hour, Radio 4, Good Friday, April 2 2010. *The World's Greatest Double Act,* Mail on Sunday Review, 10 May 2010. Fish and Chips Go Global, Waitrose Weekend, 21 October 2010.

2 Larry Zuckerman, *The Potato,* Macmillan, (1998).

3 Food History Timeline, BBC/Open University, http://web.archive.org/web/20041118084945/http://www.open2.net/everwondered_food/history/history_timeline3.htm .

4 Jonathan Brown , *Farming in Lincolnshire 1850-1945*, History of Lincolnshire Committee, (2005).

5 Whites 1856 Lincolnshire, Reprint for David and Charles, (1969), p.36.

6 William White Limited, *Lincolnshire 1872 History and Directory*, part reproduction, Introduction by Michael Winton, Hindsight Publications, (1988).

7 Christopher Awdry, *British Railway Companies*, Patrick Stephens Ltd, (1990), p.268.

8 John Wrottesley, *The Great Northern Railway, Volume 1, Origins and Developmen,* Batsford, (1979), p.159.

9 Jack Simmons, *The Railway in Town and Country 1830-1914,* David and Charles, (1986), p.218.

10 George Dow, *Great Central Volume I The Progenitors, 1813-1863*, Locomotive Publishing Co, (1959), pp.176-177.

11 Robin Leleux , *A Regional History of the Railways of Great Britain, Volume 9, The East Midlands,* David St John Thomas, Second Edition, (1984), p.216.

12 Captain J Man, 'The Grimsby Fishing Industry, *LNER Magazine*, Vol 18, No 3, (May 1928), pp.103-105.

13 VM Barrington-Ward, DSO, 'Fish Traffic', *LNER Magazine*, Vol 18, No 10, (October 1928), pp.509-512.

14 VM Barrington-Ward, DSO, 'Fish Traffic', *LNER Magazine*, Vol 18, IBID.

15 Easter Fish Traffic, *LNER Magazine*, Vol 21, No 5, (May 1931), p.232.

16 ' Record Landings of Fish at Hull and Grimsby', *LNER Magazine*, Vol 27, No 6, (June 1937), p.280.

17 A Regional History of the Railways of Great Britain, Volume 9, The East Midlands, Robin Leleux, David St John Thomas, Second Edition, 1984.

18 Port of Grimsby and Immingham, Associated British Ports, J Burrow and Co Ltd, undated.

19 Captain J Man, 'The Grimsby Fishing Industry, *LNER Magazine*, IBID.

20 GB Massa, 'Kings Cross Potato Market, LNER, *LNER Magazine*, Vol 19, No3,1929, pp.134-136.

21 Charles Dix, *The Lincolnshire Potato Traffic*, The Railway Magazine, (August 1916), pp.73-78.

22 A Munro, 'Spalding, Lincolnshire, *LNER Magazine,* Vol 22, No 4, (April 1932), pp.176-179.

23 Jonathan Brown, *Farming in Lincolnshire 1850-1945*, IBID.

24 Great Eastern Railway Society Journal Special, Number 4, *Joint Line Centenary,* (October 1982).

25 See CW Judge, *Axholme Joint Railway*, Oakwood Press, (1994).

26 http://web.archive.org/web/20080116221706/http://www.niagara.co.uk/fish_and_chips.htm.

6.1 COAL FIRED FISH AND CHIP SHOPS

Stewart Squires

Figure 6.1.1
The Upton Fish and Chip shop. The range is inside the right hand door, below the smoking chimney. *(Stewart Squires)*

At one time all fish and chip shops had ranges that were coal fired but now such ranges are very rare. One example is, at the time of writing, being rebuilt at Beamish, The Living Museum of the North. Another in the Black Country Museum at Dudley, where you can eat fish and chips fried in the shop, was until recently coal fired but has now been converted to oil. A non-working example is at the Ruddington Village Museum in Nottinghamshire and at the Abbey Pumping Station Museum in Leicester you can see a coal fired range in a mobile chip van that is occasionally demonstrated.

Nationally, however, only two privately owned shops with coal fired ranges still survive, supplying fish and chips in the way that they have done for years. One is in the north east, at Esh Winning, west of Durham. The other is in Lincolnshire, the Upton Fish Shop near Gainsborough. Until recently there was a second in Lincolnshire, at Wainfleet, and while the coal fired range here survived into the twenty first century, it has since been replaced.

The Upton shop was established in 1948, with a range built by Frank Ford of Halifax, the well known supplier of catering equipment. The building was part of what was originally a range of outbuildings serving the adjacent pair of houses. It proudly claims to serve only the best Grimsby fish and finest Lincolnshire Potatoes. It can only be psychological but the smell of coal smoke and frying fish and chips together make a mouth watering experience. The fish and chips really do taste better....

Figure 6.1.2
The Upton cooking range, of 1948 by Frank Ford of Halifax. *(Stewart Squires)*

Figure 6.1.3
The coal fire burning within the Upton range with its attendant bucket of coal. *(Stewart Squires)*

Chapter 7

CRISPS

David Taylor

Since the 1950s, crisp making has become a major British industry. More crisps are eaten in this country than in the rest of Europe put together, and in 2004 we each consumed, on average, about 150 packets a year[1]. Lincolnshire firms have made important contributions to the success of the industry, and despite questions about the healthiness of crisps in recent times, our national love affair with them remains undiminished. Crisp manufacture is thus a significant part of the Lincolnshire potato story, rather than a footnote to it.

Potato crisps were first produced on a large scale in 1920, when a grocery manager called Frank Smith formed Smith's Potato Crisps Ltd. in a converted store behind the Crown Hotel in the Cricklewood part of London. They were so popular that within a year he had to move to new premises, where he employed a staff of twelve. In 1922 Frank Smith added that great innovation, a twist of salt to be shaken over the crisps after the bag was opened. The reason for it was that publicans believed it would increase beer sales *(Figure 7.1)*. In 1929 Smith's became a public company, but it had to be rescued from voluntary liquidation by its Australian subsidiary in 1932. Despite this setback, it grew steadily and dominated a slowly expanding market until the late 1950s, when the name of Smith's became virtually synonymous with crisps[2].

Figure 7.1
Smith's Potato Crisps beer mat.
(Courtesy of Walkers Snackfoods Ltd)

Figure 7.2
The Smith's Potato Crisps factory on Newark Road, Lincoln, soon after it opened in 1938.
(Courtesy of Walkers Snackfoods Ltd)

In 1936 Frank Smith purchased the Nocton estate, approximately eight miles south of Lincoln, which had been established by William Dennis & Sons in 1919. It consisted of 8,000 acres of land, situated between Potterhanworth, Nocton and Dunston to the west and the River Witham near Bardney to the east. He envisaged using it to grow varieties of potato like *Record* that are especially suitable for making crisps, and as a guaranteed supply of raw material in emergencies. He often visited the estate, and was present at the opening of Nocton Village Hall in 1947[3].

In addition to acquiring the estate, Smith's also opened a new factory in Newark Road, Lincoln in 1938, located about a mile south of the City centre *(Figure 7.2)*. It was the first new factory to be built in Lincoln for twenty years. Potatoes were sent there by rail or lorry from a railhead adjacent to Nocton & Dunston railway station on the former Great Northern and Great Eastern Joint between Lincoln and Sleaford *(Figure 7.3)*. They were brought there from the fields by an extensive narrow gauge railway system[4]. *(See Chapter 5.1)* The Nocton Estate was managed by 'Smith's Potato

Figure 7.3
Two Albion six-wheel lorries at Nocton loaded with 1cwt sacks of potatoes for the factory in Lincoln in the 1950s.
(Courtesy of Walkers Snackfoods Ltd)

Figure 7.4
Production line workers taking washed potatoes to be peeled and sliced at Lincoln in the 1950s
(Photo courtesy of Walkers Snackfoods Ltd)

Figure 7.5
Preparing labels for tins of crisps in a Smith's factory in the 1950s (Courtesy of Walkers Snackfoods Ltd)

Estates Ltd.', and no new farming methods were introduced until the first tractors replaced horses in 1948. Mechanisation then gradually improved the growing and harvesting of potatoes, and when all the fields were linked by roads, the narrow gauge railway became redundant[5]. The last section closed in 1969. In 1960, the estate supplied between 10% and 15% of Smith's total production needs at both Lincoln and its other factories. Smith's sold the estate to an American company called General Mills in 1971, who traded in England as 'Tom Foods'. The importance of the Lincoln factory was summed up in 1965 by Mr L.A. Baker, a retired local banker, at the 13th Annual Staff Dinner, when he remarked that; 'The coming to Lincolnshire of Smith's Potato Estates has been a godsend to the County'.

The new factory of 1938 was designed by the Bristol based architect, A.E. Powell, in the art deco style favoured by Smith's for all its factories, of which there were twenty four in 1960. These were scattered throughout the country, with the Company's Head office and works based in Brentford. During the Second World War Smith's made crisps for the armed forces, and women workers were drafted in to work twelve hour shifts on tasks like unloading sacks of potatoes, washing them, feeding potatoes into slicers, packing boxes and gluing labels on to tins[6] *(Figures 7.4 and 7.5)*. Unlike sweets, crisps were never rationed. They were fried using a batch system, in which the potato slices had to be removed from the cooking oil before the next batch could be fried. In the 1950s the factory's delivery vans carried the proud slogan, 'Smith's famous potato crisps. We help to feed the Nation'. At this time they were fitted with roof racks for transporting extra tins[7] *(Figure 7.6)*.

Potato crisps have been described as the 'glamour product of the 1960s'[8], and it was during that decade they changed from being an occasional snack consumed mainly in licensed premises and on holiday, to an everyday food item especially favoured by children. The reasons for this were improved production methods, particularly the introduction of the continuous-frying cooker from America, new flavours and ambitious expansion programmes by firms like Golden Wonder. Using television advertising campaigns, Golden Wonder had captured 40% of the market by the end of the decade, whilst Smith's share dropped to 33%. However, its overall size trebled, and more crisps were

Figure 7.6
Delivery vans at the Smith's factory in Lincoln in the 1960s (Courtesy of Walkers Snackfoods Ltd)

now being sold by grocers' shops, small corner shops and in the new supermarkets than in clubs and pubs. To counter this, Smith's had reduced the number of its factories to four by 1972, when potatoes accounted for just 12% of the cost of making one of its packets of crisps. However, it still possessed a large workforce, with 600 people employed in sales and distribution alone.

In 1966 the Lincoln factory ceased making crisps altogether and was converted into a centre used solely for the manufacture of snackfoods. In 1968 its long association with 'Quavers' began, followed by the launch of 'Chipsticks' four years later. Quavers are a deep fried cheese flavoured snack, whose name comes from their resemblance to the musical note of the same name. By the 1980s, the factory was employing a workforce of around 600, which had declined to 400 in 1990.

In 1993, Smith's merged with Walkers Crisps, and after new investment at Lincoln in 1998, 300 permanent, and 120 part time staff were producing eight million packets of Quavers and three million packets of Square Crisps a week. Square Crisps were first launched in 1978, and Quavers were Walkers' biggest selling snackfood in 2010. The company was also Britain's largest crisp manufacturer, and 'Walkers Crisps' the country's biggest selling food brand. In 1998 the former England footballer, Gary Lineker made a surprise visit to the factory as part of Walkers 50th Anniversary celebrations[9].

The Newark Road factory, although an important manufacturing centre, was built in 1938 by an existing company. Riley's Potato Crisps Ltd. on the other hand, was an indigenous Lincolnshire firm, started in Scunthorpe in 1947 by two brothers called Alfred Riley (who was always known by his nickname 'Biff'), and Dennis Riley. They realised that with sweets still rationed, there was a gap in the market for a relatively easily produced snackfood. A lot of small firms started in this way, and several like Riley's went on to become major companies. Seabrooks was founded by Colin Brook at his father's fish and chip restaurant in Bradford in 1945, Golden Wonder (named after a variety of potato) was started in Edinburgh by a baker called

Figure 7.7
An early advertisement for Riley's Crisps when they were still operating from the family fish & chip shop in 72 West Street, Scunthorpe.
(Courtesy of the Tayto Group)

William Alexander in 1947, and a year later, a Leicester butcher called Henry Walker formed Walkers Crisps.

Once they had purchased a potato slicer, the Riley brothers began making crisps at their father's fish and chip shop at 72 West Street in Scunthorpe, using locally grown potatoes and the frying equipment in the shop *(Figure 7.7)*. Crisps were fried in the morning, bagged in the afternoon, and in the evening the shop reverted to selling fish and chips. At the same time they were converting a nearby warehouse behind 23 Allanby Street into a new factory which was completed in 1953. Initially they only produced plain crisps with salt wrapped in the traditional blue paper twists, but a cheese flavour was later introduced at Allanby Street. Sales and production grew and by the late 1950s the factory was using about twenty tons of potatoes a week and employed a staff of over twenty four. They were mainly women workers recruited from the adjoining terrace streets, but by this time the Allanby Street factory was becoming too small, and there were problems manufacturing in a residential area. So, with the help of the local Council's Development Officer, they moved to a new site in Colin Road, where crisp making is still thriving today[10] *(Figure 7.8)*.

From the outset, Alfred Riley was in charge of the production side of the company, whilst his brother Dennis managed sales and distribution. In the very early days, their first outlets were local pubs like the 'Comet', 'Priory' and 'Queensway' in Scunthorpe, social clubs like the 'Rabbit and Net' on Rowland Road, as well as a contract to supply public houses owned by Hewitt's brewery in Grimsby, and later Sergeant's brewery in Brigg. They then began to develop what would later become a famous system of retail van sales. This involved salesmen cold canvassing pubs, clubs and small shops in specific areas in order to build up regular delivery rounds. Personal service and Riley's reputation for quality gave it the edge over its rivals, who at that time were mainly Smith's and a firm called XL Crisps based in Conisbrough.

The crisps were packed in square tins containing eighteen packets, and sold for 4/6d a tin in the early 1960s, (4/8d

Figure 7.8
Lady operatives picking out burnt crisps from amongst the fresh ones coming out of the cooker at Riley's Colin Road factory in the 1960s. The supervisor is Mr Ken Boyd. (Courtesy of the Tayto Group)

Figure 7.9
A display of eighteen packets of crisps contained in one of Riley's tins in the 1950s. Plain crisps then cost 3d and cheese flavoured crisps 4d.
(Courtesy of the Tayto Group)

for the first cheese-flavoured crisps), with a 2/- deposit on the tin *(Figure 7.9)*. The tins were valuable items, which had to be steam cleaned when they were returned to the factory and a new label glued on, but in 1965 they were replaced by cardboard cartons which held forty-eight packets. Similar tins from the Smith's Lincoln factory were reused in 1966 to grow plants at Pennell's nursery in Brant Road, Lincoln.

Finding new customers was not an easy task, but gradually the salesmen's rounds extended from the Scunthorpe area to Grimsby and parts of Yorkshire, particularly Doncaster and York *(Figure 7.10)*. One shop in Sheffield took Riley's crisps in exchange for bottles of cockles and mussels, and a long standing contract was with the annual Scunthorpe steelworks' galas. The Lincoln area was a difficult one to break into because of the Smith's factory there[11].

As well as crisps, the Riley's vans also carried bought in confectionery, cockles and mussels, nuts, pickled onions, pickled eggs, vinegar, and, at Christmas time, puddings and mince pies supplied by Springs Jam factory in Brigg; in fact anything that would encourage landlords or shopkeepers to become part of a round. Once they began selling Riley's crisps, retailers could expect a reliable service delivered at the same time each week, as well as incentives like Riley's badges, beer mats, penknives and tin waitress trays. The advantage of the system for the company was a guaranteed flow of cash when production was slack.

Riley's were the most enthusiastic of the major manufacturers to use this method of selling, and by the 1980s they had developed a nationwide system of sixteeen retail depots with over 200 vans and twenty-four larger vehicles supplying them from the factory. The first was at Ilkeston, and eventually there were depots as far apart as Caernarvon in Wales, Coatbridge in Scotland and Eastleigh and Plymouth in the south of England. With Riley's Crisps now a national brand, retail van sales continued to be an important part of its distribution arm, even after wholesale sales increased dramatically in the 1970s.

When Riley's moved to their new factory in Colin Road, Scunthorpe, most of the staff and equipment from the old factory, including twenty-two batch fryers, went with them. The new premises lent themselves to increased production, and the first improvement was an automatic cooker. By the end of the decade, the factory had become fully automated, apart from filling hoppers with potatoes at one end of the production line and packing boxes at the other. Two production lines were in use, but they were replaced by bigger cookers and faster, more reliable machines in the 1970s. A major factor in the

Figure 7.10
Filling one of Riley's retail sales vans with tins of crisps outside their Allanby Street factory in 1956.
(Courtesy of the Tayto Group)

Figure 7.11
In the Riley's factory in the late 1970s, fresh crisps on the right are arriving by conveyor belt to be automatically weighed and filled into packets. On the left, the packets are being packed into boxes by hand.
(Courtesy of the Tayto Group)

Riley brothers' success was their willingness to invest in new technology *(Figure 7.11)*.

At the beginning of the 1960s, the market for crisps was still seasonal with the Summer holiday months the busiest period, but the company gradually began to obtain contracts to supply the new supermarkets, as well as manufacturing for smaller companies like Clockface Crisps in St. Helens, Crown Crisps in Blackpool, and Robinson's Potato Crisps in Coventry. The next decade was one of innovation and expansion as Riley's built on both the steady growth of the company and the increased popularity of crisps throughout the country. By 1980, it had captured 12% of the crisp market, and the workforce had risen from 150 to 1,100 in ten years. This was achieved by a programme of increasing sales volume and introducing new plant and machinery directed by a Cambridge economics graduate called Bob Curgenven[12]. He joined Riley's in 1972 at the tender age of 24 and in 1981 led a management buy-out which resulted in the company being renamed 'Sooner Foods'. By this time it had become the fifth largest manufacturer in Britain, but it still retained its family atmosphere. One of the company's co-owners, Alfred Riley, could usually be found on the factory floor tinkering with the production line machines!

The 1980s was a time of rapid change in the industry, as production became concentrated in the hands of fewer and fewer firms. It was inevitable that a successful company like Sooner Foods, with an experienced workforce and nationally known brand names such as 'Nik Naks' and 'Wheat Crunchies', would be seen as an attractive take-over target. This duly occurred in June 1982, when the company was bought by Rowntree Mackintosh.

The new owners invested heavily in new machinery and increased expenditure on advertising and promotions, an area in which Riley's had never been able to compete with the larger companies. Sales and profits grew and manufacturing included 'own brand' crisps for supermarkets like Safeway, Sainsbury, Tesco and Waitrose, as well as snacks for Marks & Spencer. These were often packed in 'multibags' of six or more packets.

However, after some losses, Rowntree decided that their traditional expertise in confectionery did not easily transfer to making crisps, and sold the company in 1988 to a large American food corporation called Borden International. It became their biggest snackfood manufacturing centre outside the United States, and was renamed 'Sooner Snacks' *(Figure 7.12)*. Borden continued to develop Riley's retail van sales network, even though crisps were now mainly sold through supermarkets and wholesale chains, and in 1990 the workforce reached a peak of around 1,600, mainly female employees[13]. Nevertheless, in 1992, ownership changed hands once again, when it was acquired by Golden Wonder.

Golden Wonder was an established crisp maker, formed in 1947, who had at one time been the largest in the country. After acquiring Sooner Snacks, they eventually concentrated manufacture at the Scunthorpe factory and one in Corby. New investment began in 1995, including a new factory building, but an era also ended in 1995, when 'Riley's Crisps' ceased to be used as a brand name. In 2003, the Scunthorpe factory was producing 2 million packets of crisps and 400,000 packets of 'Nik

Figure 7.12
An advertisement showing the range of products made by Sooner Foods after the takeover by Rowntree Mackintosh in 1982. (Courtesy of the Tayto Group)

Naks' a day, and they were the first company to fry crisps entirely in sunflower oil.

Despite this, Golden Wonder went into administration in early 2006, at a time when there were national concerns about rising obesity levels, particularly amongst children. Even sales of Walkers crisps, which accounted for over half the market, fell dramatically, and it led to a take over by the Northern Irish firm of Tayto Crisps, who were started by Thomas Hutchinson in Tandragee in 1956.

Tayto have retained the 'Golden Wonder' brand name, which is very popular in Scotland, and have continued to invest in the Scunthorpe factory. In 2009 it employed 300 workers, and had become the third largest crisp and snackfood manufacturer in the United Kingdom. One result of the takeover, however, was the sale of 'Nik Naks' and 'Wheat Crunchies' to K.P. Snacks. The former is a maize based extruded snack, famous for its exotic flavourings, which was first made by Sooner Foods under license in 1982. Up until then, they had only ever been manufactured in this country in Scunthorpe.

In a sense, crisp making in Lincolnshire returned to its roots in 2004, when a small independent company called 'Pipers Crisps' was formed in Elsham by three farmers, including Alex Albone. They specialise in hand-made 'kettle' cooked crisps fried in sunflower oil, and pride themselves on using only locally grown potatoes and natural ingredients *(Figure 7.13)*. By 2010, their workforce had grown to thirty full-time employees, who were producing a million packets of their prize-winning crisps a month.

They deliberately supply independent retailers, not supermarkets, with a range of exotic flavoured crisps, whose appeal is to a niche market of adult crisp connoisseurs[14]. These outlets, now numbering over 1,500, which are supplied by retail vans in exactly the

Figure 7.13
Pipers Crisps range. (Courtesy of Pipers Crisps)

Figure 7.14
Alex Albone, the Managing Director of Pipers Crisps.
(Courtesy of Pipers Crisps)

same way the Riley brothers did when they started out in business over 60 years earlier. Small firms like Pipers are the crisp making equivalent of microbreweries in the brewing industry *(Figure 7.14)*.

In 2011, crisp and associated snackfood manufacture is still an important Lincolnshire industry, with two major centres in Lincoln and Scunthorpe and an emerging young company in Elsham. The Lincoln factory is now the oldest in the country and the history of the old Riley's factory in Scunthorpe accurately reflects the many changes that have taken place in the industry since the Second World War. Their success underlines how important potato growing is to the local economy, and of course, our continuing appetite for the humble crisp.

Endnotes

1 In 2004, 430,000 tonnes of crisps were sold in the United Kingdom, with a retail value of £4bn. The Snack, Nut and Crisp Manufacturers Association.

2 B.B.C. Home website, '*Potato Crisps – A history*', 7 December 2006.

3 Sheila Redshaw and Sue Morris, '*Nocton. The Last Years of an Estate Village. Volume One*' Tucann Books 2007.

4 Stewart E.Squires, '*The Lincolnshire Potato Railways*' The Oakwood Press, 1987.

5 Len Woodhead, '*A Lincolnshire lad looks back. Nocton Estate. The home of Smith's Crisps*' Japonica Press, 2003.

6 Linda Crust (ed), '*Ration books and rabbit pie. Lincolnshire folk remember the War*', Society for Lincolnshire History and Archaeology, 2008.

7 Len Woodhead, '*A Lincolnshire lad's scrapbook. More tales from Nocton Estate*' , Japonica Press, 2008.

8 Alan Bevan, The U.K. potato crisp industry, 1960-72: A study of new entry competition, *The Journal of Industrial Economics*, June 1974.

9 Information from Walkers Snackfoods Ltd. in Lincoln.

10 Interview with Alfred Riley in 2004.

11 Much of the information about Riley's Potato Crisps Ltd. and its successor companies is taken from interviews with 17 former employees conducted by North Lincolnshire Museum in 2004.

12 'Riley's forge ahead', *Snackfood Manufacture & Marketing'*, Summer 1981.

13 'Sooner Snacks. Putting people first', *Business Link,* February 1990.

14 This is Scunthorpe website, 'Increase in orders leads to Pipers Crisps doubling its production capacity' 2 July 2010.

Chapter 8

INTO THE FREEZER

Catherine Wilson

Ensuring a year-round supply of fresh food, particularly vegetables, was a significant challenge before the twentieth century. In the UK techniques such as air-drying, smoking, and salting were used to preserve meat and fish, whilst fruit and vegetables could be made into jams, pickles and chutneys, but generally whole vegetables do not keep well once harvested. At the beginning of the nineteenth century a process of preserving food by canning was developed by Peter Durand, a British merchant, who received a patent for it in 1810 (Patent Number 3372). Canning techniques improved significantly throughout the nineteenth century, and became cheaper, so that tinned food, particularly vegetables, became available to everyone and this was really the first 'convenience' food. However, the process of canning changes the taste and the texture of food. Freezing, on the other hand, preserves both the look and the taste of the fresh product, and preserves its nutritional content.

Figure 8.1
Supermarkets supplied by PAS (Grantham) Limited.
(PAS publicity brochure)

Experiments with freezing food started in America towards the end of the nineteenth century but it was Clarence Birdseye who developed the first successful quick-freezing process. He was born in Brooklyn, New York in 1886 and spent sometime as a fur trader in Labrador, Canada, where he observed that fish caught by the Inuit of the Arctic froze instantly on being taken from the water and, when thawed out months later, still tasted fresh. He concluded that it was the speed of the freezing which preserved the taste and texture and set about developing a process which could be used commercially. He succeeded in this and the first quick frozen vegetables and other products were sold to the public in 1930.[1]

However, the widespread acceptance of frozen products depended on shops having freezers to store them in, and on the ready availability of fridges and freezers in the home, so it was several years before they became widely available. World War II provided an impetus to frozen food as the metal used for canning was more urgently needed for armaments and by the 1950s consumers were becoming accustomed to frozen products. In Lincolnshire, Grimsby became a centre for frozen foods with facilities for freezing both fish and vegetables and with both Ross Foods and Bird's Eye establishing substantial factories. Peas were, and still are, one of the most popular vegetables for freezing and many Lincolnshire farmers grew vining peas for the Grimsby factories. Frozen potatoes came rather later and it was not until the 1960s that the freezing of potato chips was perfected in America.

Today one of the largest suppliers of frozen potato products in the country is **PAS (Grantham) Ltd,** now part of the McCain group of companies. I am indebted to **Richard Harris OBE**, for explaining how this came about.

PAS (Potato & Allied Services) was formed from an initiative by two local farmers Jim Bealby and Tony Keen who, in the 1960s, grew 800 acres of potatoes and a substantial acreage of peas between them. They were considering how they could create a better market for the potatoes they were producing when they met Bill Pellew-Harvey who had started importing frozen chips from America. The three of them saw the potential for building a chip factory in the UK. They then visited America to see how the process worked there and to meet the American producers. It was decided to form a company to build and run a new frozen chip factory in Britain and this became known as PAS (Potato and Allied Services). The Americans, who supplied the necessary machinery and 'know-how', took 40% shares, Bill Pellew-Harvey 20%, with Jim Bealby and Tony Keen having 40%.

A chance meeting with Peter Whitton of Escritt & Barrell, Estate Agents, elicited the information that the Cholmondley Estate was selling an old ironstone mine at Easton, near Grantham. This site was considered suitable as it had a good a source of water, it was close to a good road network and had land suitable for building. Jim Bealby and Tony Keen bought the site and then sold it to Christian Salvesen, who wanted to develop a cold storage complex there and were willing to provide the refrigeration needed for chip factory. Thus the factory was built and production commenced in 1969/70, with Richard Harris as its first General Manager.

Unfortunately significant problems with the site subsequently became apparent, particularly regarding effluent from the potato processing plant, which required extra investment. The original shareholders were unable to provide this and there was disagreement about the way forward. To resolve the situation Christian Salvesen, who by this time were running a successful cold storage business on the site, acquired the processing plant and took over the running of PAS in 1972. They developed and expanded this part of the business, building it up to become the second largest frozen chip producer in country, second only to McCain.

Figure 8.2
A selection of the frozen potato products produced by PAS.
(PAS publicity brochure)

The chip market was expanding rapidly with a significant increase in demand as consumers realised the convenience of the product. McCain were anxious to break into the private label market (this is the term used for supermarkets' 'own brand' products) in which PAS were dominant. Meanwhile Christian Salvesen, which had come into the frozen chip market by accident, wanted to concentrate on its core business of cold storage and transport. So in 1982 McCain acquired the potato processing plant at Easton. They re-employed all staff and renamed it PAS (Grantham) Ltd. McCain have continued to invest and expand the company and it has gone from strength to strength. Initial production capacity was 20,000 tons per annum; the current capacity is 175,000 tons per annum, an increase of 155,000 tons, or 20% per annum. The company currently employs 350 people, most of whom are recruited locally, so it is very significant to the economy of the Grantham area.

McCain started in Canada where the company is still based but it is now a multi-national company with sixty-three manufacturing sites worldwide including at Scarborough and Whittlesey in the UK. It provides most of the chips for McDonalds as well as its own branded products. What makes PAS special is that it is a wholly owned subsidiary, retaining its own identity, filing its own accounts and producing a product that is not sold under the McCain label. Instead PAS produce 40% of the frozen processed potato products sold as 'own label' by most of country's supermarkets, including Marks & Spencer, Waitrose, Tesco and Asda *(Figure 8.1)*. The range of products has also expanded considerably so that PAS now supply not just chips but curly fries, hash browns, ready roast, crinkle cut and wedges, products which year on year are becoming an increasingly large part of national potato sales *(Figure 8.2)*.

The process for producing these tasty and convenient products is fairly straightforward. Some potatoes are bought on contract but most are 'free buy' on the open market. There are long-standing relationships with most of the growers though the quantity bought and the price paid will vary from year to year. The potatoes are sourced from all over the country, but a significant percentage comes from the local area. The main varieties used are *Maris Piper*, *Desiree*, *Pentland Dell* and *King Edward*. It was PAS who first used *Maris Piper* for frozen chips.

Figure 8.3
Coated potato wedges produced by PAS
(PAS publicity brochure)

Ensuring a steady and reliable supply is important to keep the production line busy and to meet the needs of customers. The grower cleans and de-stones the potatoes and stores them in standard bulk bins. They are then transferred to PAS as needed. On arriving at PAS the potatoes are sorted and washed; their starch content is checked and a sample is fried to test the end colour and determine cooking time for different varieties. They are peeled by high-pressure steam; the production line machinery then takes them through the following processes: they are trimmed, preheated, cut to the desired shape, sorted optically for blemishes, blanched, dried, fried at the right temperature and for the right time; then pre-cooled, frozen and packed into appropriate bags depending on customers' requirements. A metal detector scans all bags to ensure there are no 'foreign bodies' and there is quality control throughout the entire process, which takes about one and a half hours from washing to freezing. The process is reasonably straightforward, but there is considerable skill in ensuring that the end product is consistent and meets the specifications of the different buyers, from the 'value' end of the market to the retailers who require higher quality.

The bags of frozen products are put into polythene pouches, then into boxes and immediately transferred

Figure 8.4
The sorting and grading line at Branston. (Branston Ltd.)

Figure 8.5
Part of the quality control process at Branston, eliminating green or damaged potatoes. (Branston Ltd.)

to refrigerated storage on site, prior to transport to supermarket distribution centres across the country. There is a supply chain of about three weeks – PAS store a week's supply whilst the supermarkets have a one to two week's supply *(Figure 8.3)*.[2]

Whilst the main buildings at PAS are basically the same as they were in the 1970s and the processes have not changed fundamentally, new plant has been installed over the years with an investment of some £20 million to make the plant more efficient and able to cope with the greatly increased and varied demand.

From the ideas of two Lincolnshire farmers in the 1960s, PAS (Grantham) Ltd has grown to be one of the most important potato processing sites in the country, producing as it does some 20% of the country's frozen potato products.

Endnote

1 Mary Bellis, *Frozen Foods – Clarence Birdseye, (http://inventors*.about.com./library/inventors/blfrd.htm).

2 I am grateful to David Chelley of PAS for taking me on a tour of the site.

Chapter 9

POTATO MARKETING

Charles Parker

In 1860, 80% of food consumed in the UK was produced locally but by the 1870s this had declined due to a series of bad harvests and the arrival of cheaper imports from abroad. Prices paid to farmers fell and agriculture entered a depression that lasted for nearly thirty years. By 1900 over half of the food consumed in Britain was imported. The First World War focused public attention on the importance of agriculture and legislation was passed to stimulate home production. However, this was short-lived and in the years following the war farmers faced widely fluctuating markets and often disastrously low returns. In 1930, for instance, there is evidence of many thousands of tons of potatoes left to rot down or sold very cheaply at the farm.

The wider uncertainties facing agriculture as a whole led to the introduction of Government measures to support sugar beet, wheat, cattle, dairy and sheep. The Agricultural Marketing Acts of 1931 and 1933 were passed to allow groups of producers to prepare schemes for the marketing of their crops and, if these schemes were approved by a substantial majority of growers, they were made enforceable under the authority of Parliament. The second part of this legislation covered the restriction of imported agricultural produce, regulation of the quantity of corresponding home-grown products sold in the United Kingdom, and compensation payments and guarantees. The control of imports of main crop potatoes to protect British growers would become a key factor in the operation of the Potato Marketing Scheme.

Potato producers had suffered particularly from fluctuating prices, since sales did not increase as prices fell. Potatoes were a staple part of the British diet and demand from the public is almost totally unaffected by price. Crop yields vary from year to year dependent on growing conditions and acreage planted. Thus in a season when there was adequate rainfall through the growing

Figure 9.1
The Potato Marketing Board logo changed over the years. Their first was the roundel with an intertwined PMB in the centre. The second showed the potato plant in the ground. The final one had the sun rising over a rolling landscape, perhaps reflecting the way growing was now taking place within landscapes other than the Fens. *(Charles Parker Collection)*

period and harvesting conditions were good, growers could hope for a bumper crop, but if this led to over supply then prices were depressed. Conversely, a poor growing season with either drought, too much rain or a wet harvest often created shortages and the price rose accordingly. The commercial success of one season often affected the acreage planted the following year and this also had an effect on prices. Therefore potato growers were among the first to see the benefits of the Agricultural Marketing Acts, and a scheme was drafted which, as the Potato Marketing Scheme (Approval) Order, received the approval of Parliament on 20th December, 1933.

The Potato Marketing Board (PMB) took its full powers in March 1934 *(Figure 9.1)*. Their powers were, however, limited: there was no system of price support but the Board had the powers to impose a levy on the area planted and control plantings in excess of a basic allocation. The aim was to stabilise the acreage of potatoes planted every year and stop the wide fluctuations that had taken place in the past. This, along with regulations on the size of potatoes offered for sale and licensing of selected reputable merchants, introduced a measure of stability which producers had not enjoyed previously. At the outbreak of World War II in 1939 the Board's activities were suspended and control of the industry passed to the Ministry of Food who took over its staff and equipment.

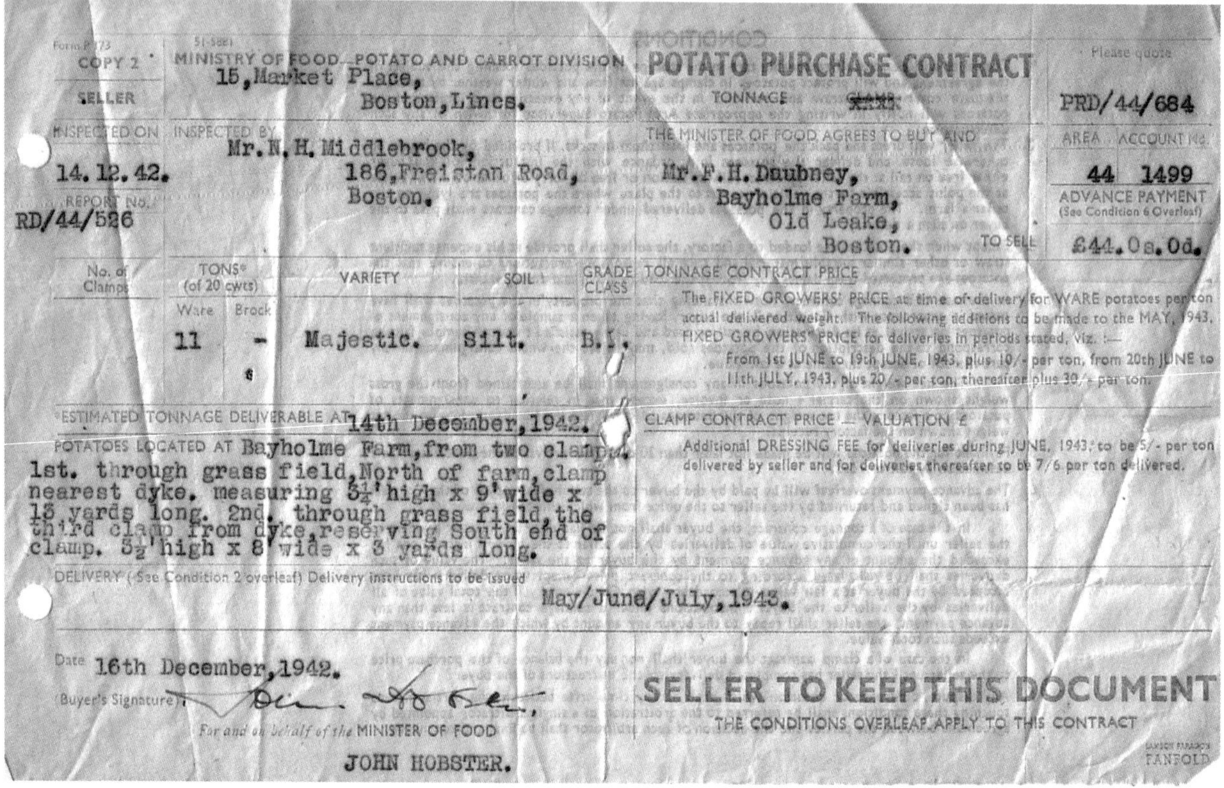

COPY 2
MINISTRY OF FOOD—POTATO AND CARROT DIVISION
POTATO PURCHASE CONTRACT

SELLER: 15, Market Place, Boston, Lincs.

TONNAGE ~~CLAMP~~ — Please quote PRD/44/684

INSPECTED ON: 14.12.42.
INSPECTED BY: Mr. N. H. Middlebrook, 186, Freiston Road, Boston.
REPORT No.: RD/44/526

THE MINISTER OF FOOD AGREES TO BUY AND Mr. F. H. Daubney, Bayholme Farm, Old Leake, Boston. TO SELL

AREA: 44 ACCOUNT No.: 1499
ADVANCE PAYMENT (See Condition 6 Overleaf): £44.0s.0d.

No. of Clamps	TONS (of 20 cwts) Ware	Brock	VARIETY	SOIL	GRADE CLASS
	11	-	Majestic.	Silt.	B.I.

TONNAGE CONTRACT PRICE
The FIXED GROWERS' PRICE at time of delivery for WARE potatoes per ton actual delivered weight. The following additions to be made to the MAY, 1943, FIXED GROWERS' PRICE for deliveries in periods stated, viz. :—
From 1st JUNE to 19th JUNE, 1943, plus 10/- per ton, from 20th JUNE to 11th JULY, 1943, plus 20/- per ton, thereafter plus 30/- per ton.

ESTIMATED TONNAGE DELIVERABLE AT 14th December, 1942.

CLAMP CONTRACT PRICE — VALUATION £
Additional DRESSING FEE for deliveries during JUNE, 1943, to be 5/- per ton delivered by seller and for deliveries thereafter to be 7/6 per ton delivered.

POTATOES LOCATED AT Bayholme Farm, from two clamps. 1st. through grass field, North of farm, clamp nearest dyke, measuring 3½' high x 9' wide x 15 yards long. 2nd. through grass field, the third clamp from dyke, reserving South end of clamp. 5½' high x 8' wide x 3 yards long.

DELIVERY (See Condition 2 overleaf) Delivery instructions to be issued May/June/July, 1943.

Date 16th December, 1942.
(Buyer's Signature)
For and on behalf of the MINISTER OF FOOD
JOHN HOBSTER.

SELLER TO KEEP THIS DOCUMENT
THE CONDITIONS OVERLEAF APPLY TO THIS CONTRACT

Figure 9.2
A Potato Purchase Contract of 1942, issued on behalf of the Minister of Food to Mr F.H. Daubney of Old Leake. This was for 11 tons of ware (maincrop) potatoes, for delivery in May/June/July 1943. The very detailed description of the dimensions and locations of the two clamps from which they were to be taken indicates both the level of control of the market and the creation of what we would now call an audit trail.
(Courtesy of the Daubney family)

DIG FOR VICTORY
LEAFLET No. 17

POTATO BLIGHT

BLIGHT attacks potatoes when the weather is warm, wet and muggy, and may kill the tops as early as the end of July or the beginning of August. If this happens, not only is the yield reduced, but the tubers may become infected and rot in the ground, or in storage.

Spraying will protect the tops from blight, if it is properly done, and care at lifting time will protect the tubers from infection. In time of war, when maximum production is essential, every allotment holder and gardener (except those in smoky industrial districts) should consider spraying his maincrop potatoes as an insurance against blight. And all growers, without exception, should take precautions to avoid infection of the tubers at digging time. These instructions will help growers to get good disease-free crops.

What to Spray

Early varieties usually do not need spraying, as they are generally lifted before blight makes its appearance. Mid-season and late varieties, however, should be sprayed, especially the varieties British Queen, King Edward and Up-to-Date, which are very susceptible to the disease.

Spraying should not be done within 10 or 12 miles of large industrial centres, for acid fumes in the smoke may react with the spray and cause injury to the plants.

If in doubt, ask the secretary of your allotment society to obtain information, or ask your local horticultural committee.

The Spray to Use

There are three kinds of spray from which to choose:

READY-MADE SPRAY MIXTURES. There are numbers of these on the market. Some are sold as Bordeaux powders or pastes. Others are given special names. They have only to be mixed with water according to the instructions given on the tins or packets. For this reason they are more convenient to prepare than the home-made mixtures, and there are a number of brands on the market that give very good results. When made up with water, the best sprays show little sign of settling after they have been standing for an hour.

HOME-MADE BORDEAUX MIXTURE. This is made from bluestone (sulphate of copper), hydrated lime and water. The bluestone should be 98 per cent. pure, and it is best to buy either the powdered or granular form as these dissolve much more readily in water. The hydrated lime *must be fresh;* it can be purchased in small quantities and is more convenient to use than quick lime, as well as being free from grit.

The quantities to use are :—

bluestone	4 oz.
hydrated lime	5 oz.
water	2½ gal.

This amount of spray is sufficient to treat the potatoes on about 2 rods of ground, or rather less when the haulm is big.

Measure out 2½ gallons of water into a bucket or other container. A wooden, earthenware or enamelled vessel is best, but a galvanised bucket may be used if it is well washed afterwards. Pour off about a quart of the water into an earthenware or enamelled jug and stir into this the 4 oz. of bluestone. (Bluestone must never be put into metal vessels unprotected by enamel). While it is dissolving, shake the 5 oz. of hydrated lime into the water remaining in the bucket and stir well.

Finally, when all the copper sulphate has dissolved, slowly pour the blue solution from the jug into the milk of lime in the bucket, stirring well all the time. The sky-blue colour of Bordeaux Mixture appears at once, and the spray is then ready to apply. It should always be used the day it is made. It is best to pour it into the sprayer through a fine gauge strainer or a piece of muslin, to prevent any grit or other impurities from clogging the nozzle. Immediately after use, rinse

Figure 9.3
Dig For Victory Leaflet No 17, issued during the Second World War as one of a series of 20 leaflets giving advice on the growing of vegetables.
(Charles Parker Collection)

The Government realised that food shortages were a distinct possibility and it tackled this in two ways. War Agricultural Executive Committees were appointed for each county with wide ranging powers to drive increased production, and farmers were encouraged to expand their potato plantings by a payment of £10.00 per acre. Previously uncultivated land was ploughed up and the Ministry introduced cropping direction and price control. At the end of the war the acreage of potatoes planted was roughly double that in 1939 *(Figure 9.2)*. Additionally, in October 1939 the 'Dig for Victory' campaign was launched *(Figure 9.3)*. People were urged to use their gardens, and every spare piece of land, such as parks, golf clubs and tennis courts, was converted into allotments to grow vegetables. Good quality seed potatoes and fertiliser were made available through allotment associations to ensure that allotment holders could produce healthy crops. This scheme was very successful and the number of allotments rose from 815,000 in 1939 to 1,400,000 by 1943.

Another facet of this programme was to encourage people to eat healthy produce. Potatoes and carrots were in relatively plentiful supply and so they were widely used as a substitute for more scarce foods. An information campaign was launched with the introduction of cartoon characters called 'Potato Pete' and 'Doctor Carrot'. 'Potato Pete' also had a song to amplify its message. With vocals by Betty Driver (well known later as Betty Williams in 'Coronation Street'), the recording was a great success and did a tremendous amount of good in getting the message across. 'Potato Pete' recipe books were also written to give women suggestions and advice on how best to serve potatoes at mealtimes *(See also Chapter 12 and Figures 9.4 and 9.5)*. For example, 'scrubbing instead of peeling potatoes' was recommended, thus avoiding unnecessary wastage. Even traditional nursery rhymes were adapted to give a 'Potato Pete' theme.

The need to supply the population with a staple part of its diet brought with it the concept of the guaranteed market, which was reinforced after the war by the passing of the Agriculture Act, 1947. Potatoes were finally freed from Ministry control in 1955 when a

Figure 9.4
The Potato Recipes booklet that introduced 'Potato Pete' to the public, published in 1936.
(Catherine Wilson collection via Ken Hollamby)

Figure 9.5
Potato Pete out shopping. An example of the Potato Pete cartoons. More examples can be found in Chapter 12.
(Catherine Wilson collection via Ken Hollamby)

revised Potato Marketing Scheme was submitted to producers, confirmed by a public inquiry and ratified by Parliament. This scheme remained in place with minor amendments for over forty years.

The new Potato Marketing Board's (PMB) principal aim was to bring about assured markets and price benefits for potato growers while ensuring that production was adequate to meet home demand. In order to do this all potato producers had to register with the Board and they were allotted an acreage of potatoes that they were permitted to plant (Quota). The potato market itself remained free with a chain of distribution from the grower, through the merchant to the retailer or processor and thence to the consumer. Sales of potatoes by unregistered producers (unless they planted less than one acre) were prohibited and quality, description, and grading standards were prescribed. Growers paid a levy based on their plantings, which covered the administration of the Scheme and contributed to a Market Support Fund. Producers could grow as many potatoes as they wanted but, to discourage over-production, a penal levy was charged on any plantings in excess of their Quota. Potato buyers, agents and grower-salesmen had to be licensed and had to submit returns, estimates and other information to the Board, whose staff had the power to carry out inspections on producers' and merchants' premises to ensure compliance with the Scheme. Non-compliance could lead to the imposition of penalties on producers who knowingly or recklessly made false returns, failed to make returns or obstructed PMB staff. Using this disciplinary system, which was similar to those adopted by many forms of association, professional bodies and societies, prosecution for a breach of regulations was avoided. Similarly, the high costs of legal action were largely eliminated. Any penalties imposed became a civil debt to the Board which could be pursued through the courts.

One of the key features of the post-war scheme was the system of market support. The Government recognised that even in peacetime, potatoes were a key part of the British diet and it was essential that producers had the incentive to plant sufficient to supply the demands. Plantings were controlled so that, given yields in line with trends from previous crop years, the quantity of potatoes required to meet expected demand would be produced. The area planted each year was determined by the Government in consultation with the Board. The aim was to ensure that there was an adequate supply but, at the same time, limit the extent to which public funds were required to meet the guarantee. Britain consumed almost seven million tons of potatoes in 1955 and, apart from small quantities of early potatoes which were landed before home grown varieties were ready, it would have been impossible to import sufficient foreign main crop potatoes to meet any major shortages.

At the same time, any significant surplus would distort the market and could have a catastrophic effect on prices. The PMB gave a guarantee in the form of a 'floor' price at which it was obliged to accept all potatoes offered to it, provided they were of marketable quality. This was underwritten by the Ministry of Agriculture, Fisheries & Food (MAFF). In this way, a level was set for prices to be offered by merchants and wholesalers. A Market

Support Fund was set up and a system of deficiency payments was introduced, to be paid if average prices over a season were lower than the cost of production. Subject to minor amendments from time to time, these arrangements remained in force for over twenty years.

In later years the system was changed in order to limit the PMB's financial exposure. A series of contracts were signed by producers before the start of the season for fixed tonnages of potatoes to be delivered in monthly batches. If the market price fell below a 'trigger price', then the Board would announce that it could accept deliveries on these contracts and producers who were having difficulty selling on the open market could start dressing potatoes. Generally, these were inspected at the farm, covered with a non-toxic dye to prevent resale and sold in bulk for animal stockfeed. Most of this traffic went from the potato producing areas in eastern England to Wales and the West Country. This was a major operation for the PMB staff assessing and dying the crop on the farm and organising transport. Alternatively, the potatoes could be sent to processors for dehydration so that they could be stored or exported in flaked or powdered form. In the 1960s trials were also carried out using steamers on farms to produce cooked stockfeed, but this did not prove practical in the long term and the idea was dropped *(Figure 9.6)*. If the market remained healthy or producers could find a buyer for their crop then they were released from their contractual obligations. Regular stock returns were submitted by producers through the winter and spring so that the Board could assess whether there was any likelihood of a surplus at the end of the maincrop storage phase.

Figure 9.6
The experimental mobile potato steamer trialled in Lincolnshire about 1964. Manufactured by Gotthardt and Kuhne of Nurnberg in Germany, it was not a success. (Courtesy The Potato Council)

Acreage returns were the foundation of the Board's statistics and in order to check that they were accurate there was an annual programme of physical checking of the growers' crops. This was carried out on a parish by parish basis so that, by a process of elimination, any producers of potatoes who failed to register could be discovered. The percentage checked varied from year to year but all growers in any county would be checked over a cycle of 3-4 years. This was the key part of the scheme as it was funded by the registered producers paying an annual contribution based on their planted acreage. Towards the end of the maincrop growing season, field staff also carried out crop check yield tests on selected farms which consisted of digging up standard lengths of rows and the potato tubers were weighed by reference to a number of different riddle sizes. This information was compared with similar data obtained in previous years which gave an indication of the season's likely average yield for the country as a whole or for a single variety. Over the years as crop husbandry improved and yield per acre increased the acreage approved for planting was progressively reduced to keep the total tonnage lifted in line with demand. The control of imports of main crop potatoes remained a key factor in the operation of the Scheme as it prevented home growers being undercut by cheaper imports which would have led in turn to the Board having to buy more surplus potatoes. However, once Britain joined the European Union it became increasingly difficult to prevent imports from fellow EU members.

Figure 9.7
Potato Marketing Board demonstration at East Kirkby on 10 September, 1991. Farmers are inspecting a Grimme DLE 1700 Pick up Loader.
(Museum of English Rural Life)

Figure 9.8
Potato harvesting machinery demonstration, East Kirkby, September 1991. Seen here is the Keyag Converter, manufactured by Key Agriculture Ltd.
(Museum of English Rural Life)

The standard of merchants authorised to buy potatoes on the farm was considered equally as important as the growers themselves. In order to qualify for a Ware Merchant's licence they had to be able to show that they had experience of the wholesale ware potato trade and had a good reputation. Most importantly, they had to demonstrate that they were financially sound. Many growers had been caught out when merchants who had taken potatoes on credit got into financial difficulties or ceased trading abruptly, often because their own customers were unsound. A similar set of regulations governed Seed Potato Merchants and many of the PMB's field staff were qualified to inspect seed potatoes as well as ware. Market intelligence was considered very important and licensed potato merchants were contacted regularly to check that they were complying with their obligations. Their monthly returns were an important tool for calculating national yields and consumption and these figures were used in the process of setting the acreage planted in the following year. In addition, the price information from their returns fed into the food section of the Retail Price Index. Merchants were reviewed regularly and failure to make regular returns, comply with the terms and conditions, or most importantly, fail to pay producers could lead to the loss of their licence, which would have a serious effect on their reputation in the trade. Any complaints about a merchant's conduct by registered producers would be investigated by a member of the Merchant's Audit team and reports were sent to the Licensing Committee.

The Board also organised planting and harvesting demonstrations to give producers the opportunity to observe the latest potato machinery in action and to offer sound, practical criticism of its design and performance. This was also helpful to, and appreciated by, manufacturers as the demonstrations served as an incentive for them to compete with their rivals in efficient design. Therefore, without directly assisting any particular commercial interest, the Board took an active part in the development of new products. Arrangements were also made for the display of grading machinery and mechanical handling for all stages during storage and dressing. Performance Assessment Trials were conducted and the results, assessed by expert judges, were published on site. These demonstrations were rotated around the major potato growing areas of England and Scotland to allow the maximum numbers of growers, dealers and other potential users to attend. In September 1991 a major harvesting demonstration was held on an old airfield at East Kirkby near Spilsby *(Figures 9.7 and 9.8)*. The event was supported by Dalgety Produce, who utilised some of the old RAF hangars for storage and packing potatoes. Eighteen months later a spring potato planting demonstration was held at Grange de Lings, just north of Lincoln.

Publicity was an extremely important part of the Board's work. This had two main objectives: the promotion of the potato as an attractive and desirable food with a view to stimulating consumption; and giving the producer, the trade and the public generally a proper understanding of the aims, objectives and activities of the PMB.

It was achieved by direct advertising of potatoes and point-of-sale publicity material, for example wall charts and posters for retailers (*see Frontispiece*). Cookery demonstrations were given to ladies' groups, and on stands at agricultural shows, exhibitions and food fairs. The PMB also produced recipe books, catering manuals, advisory publications, educational aids, leaflets, selected diets and films, held press conferences and gave out news releases and articles *(Figures 9. 9 and 9.10)*. As potatoes are a staple food, it was felt that exhortations to 'eat more potatoes' would be pointless so the campaigns concentrated on the use of the potato on more occasions. Leaflets such as 'Help Yourself to Better Health' were produced in conjunction with the Health Education Council, *(Figure 9.11)* and slogans such as 'Pop on some Potatoes' were intended to suggest ease of preparation and readiness for use at any time of day. The campaigns were also designed to indicate the acceptability of properly prepared potato dishes and to counteract the widespread belief that potatoes are unduly fattening.

Newspaper, magazine and television advertising was used in years of surplus with a view to stimulating consumption, and when colour advertisements were inserted in women's magazines depicting attractive potato dishes and inviting applications for free recipe leaflets a heavy response indicated the effectiveness of this medium. Commercial television was first utilised in 1965 when an advertising film with potato chips as its theme was shown during the tea-time period. In later years direct advertising had to be curtailed for economic reasons, but with the introduction of stricter drinking-and-driving laws in 1967, the opportunity was taken to undertake a short campaign, directed towards licensees, pointing out the advantages of serving potato snacks in public houses, and to support the printed advertisements by commercial television advertising.

The Board itself was made up of eighteen elected representatives plus special members appointed by the Minister for Agriculture. These ordinary members were elected by a poll of registered producers in their area and they served for a period of four years. Elections were rotated over the intervening years to maintain a level of continuity and in practice many members had sufficient support from their electors to serve for quite long periods. The Special Members were drawn from people outside the industry with experience in commerce, public administration or labour relations to provide specialist advice in these fields. About 11% of all potatoes grown in the UK (excluding Northern Ireland) are planted in Lincolnshire and its importance as a growing area was reflected by the fact that it had two Board Members: one for the pre-1974 area of Lindsey and one to cover Kesteven and Holland.

Figure 9.9
Country Collection, a cookery book containing over 200 potato recipes, published for the Potato Marketing Board in 1977.
(Charles Parker collection)

Figure 9.11
A booklet of family recipes produced by the Potato Marketing Board in conjunction with the Health Education Council, about 1980.
(Charles Parker collection)

Figure 9.10
A booklet of potato recipes, published by the Potato Marketing Board in the 1980s.
(Charles Parker collection)

Some of these members have played major roles in the development of the industry, for example Thomas Worth of Lutton Marsh was involved in setting up the original Board in 1933. The Worth family have been major potato growers for many years; and their interest continues into the twenty first century. At the time of writing, Duncan Worth, Managing Director of A. H. Worth and Co. Ltd. of Holbeach Hurn is a Member of the Potato Council, and Thomas Worth was his great uncle.

Geoffrey Grantham *(Figure 9.12),* who now lives in Woodhall Spa, started farming in the Chapel Hill/ Walcot area in 1954 and grew 100 acres of potatoes in 1956. He was first elected to the Board in 1966 and became Vice Chairman four years later. In 1973 he became Chairman of the Board, a position that he held for ten years. After Geoffrey retired, Jim Epton was elected to represent the south of the county, a position that he held for ten years. Jim grew potatoes around Wainfleet and Croft Marsh and he had been on the National Farmers Union (NFU) Potato Committee. For part of this time, he was Chairman of the Sutton Bridge Management Committee and took an active interest in the promotion of high quality potatoes for pre-packing for sale both at home and abroad.

Jim Godfrey OBE is a Director of a long established farming business based at Elsham Top near Brigg. His father, uncle and grandfather were potato growers so it was natural that he followed them into the family business *(see Chapter 3).* He was Chairman of the Lincolnshire NFU Potato Committee and in 1988 became the local PMB Board Member for the north of the county. He was elected chairman of the Board in 1992 and later became chairman of the Scottish Crop Research Institute which has an important role in the development of new varieties. He was also chairman of the PMB's Research & Development Committee and initiated the review and subsequent refurbishment of the Sutton Bridge research operation *(see Chapter 10),* which preceded its establishment as a separate entity when the British Potato Council was formed.

At a local level there were Area Offices in Brigg (West Lindsey), Louth (East Lindsey), Sleaford (Kesteven) and Spalding (Holland), each run by an Area Supervisor with a team of Area Assistants, Fieldsmen and administrative staff. Details of all the registered producers that had any land in the area were maintained. As many of the larger growers held land in several different PMB areas it was important to maintain detailed records and liaise with all of the other Area Offices involved to ensure that planting returns were accurate. The Area Offices were overseen by a Divisional Supervisor who was also based in Sleaford.

In the 1980s pressures began to emerge for changes to the system. With its origins in the wartime Ministry of Food, the Potato Marketing Board was increasingly seen as anachronistic, with its detailed prescriptive resolutions and intrusive inspection regime, and no longer relevant to an industry which was changing rapidly. Increased mechanisation on the farm and major capital investment in storage facilities led to a rapid

Figure 9.12
Geoffrey Grantham meeting Edward Heath in 1975.
(Geoffrey Grantham Collection)

decline in the number of producers (down from over 76,000 nationally in 1960 to less than 10,000 when the PMB was wound up). Processed products in the form of frozen chips, crisps, snack foods, take-aways and ready meals began to replace traditional mashed potato or chips prepared at home, and trade in 25kg paper bags fell significantly as supermarkets demanded pre-packed washed potatoes in polythene bags. At the same time, dishes such as pasta, pizza and rice became more popular, replacing potato based meals, particularly for younger consumers. Efficient growers felt that the system of intervention buying supported the more inefficient ones at their expense, while controls on the acreage grown sometimes meant that they could not make best use of their capital investment. This view was supported by the food processors. They felt that the scheme restricted their ability to buy as much raw material as they needed if there was a shortage of suitable potatoes locally and the acreage levy added a premium of approximately £2 to the price of a tonne of potatoes. Once Britain joined the European Union it became difficult to restrict main crop imports and by the late 1980s processing quality potatoes could be bought and shipped to east coast ports as cheaply as the home grown product.

The more forward-looking Board members and staff realised that a major overhaul was needed to reflect changes in the industry with increased emphasis on improving the quality of the crop, publicity to combat competition from alternative foods, new varieties and increased research and development. Also, it needed to be much more broadly based. As a body elected by producers to represent their interests and support production it did not reflect the wider interests of the industry as a whole and the function of buyers, especially the food processors, was becoming much more important. Some growers also resented paying the levy when the majority of the PMB's income was used to administer the scheme while the amount used for intervention and market support was diminishing. One of the main functions of the organisation was to deal with surplus potatoes during buying programmes and with fewer, more efficient growers this intervention became less frequent. Between 1989 and 1993 the area offices at Brigg, Spalding and Louth closed and it became a regional operation managed from Sleaford. The 1992 crop was the last one supported by a buying programme and prices were considerably lower than in previous years. Over the next few years, Quota arrangements were phased out and growers were left free to grow as much as they wished.

The Government also took the view that agricultural marketing boards were no longer appropriate in the 1990s and in 1997 the Potato Marketing Board was wound up to be replaced by the British Potato Council. In 2008 it was renamed the Potato Council and merged with other similar levy-funded organisations to form the Agriculture and Horticulture Development Board, but still operates as a distinct organisation. The new organisation has fifteen elected members and its primary objectives are research and development and the transfer of this knowledge down the supply chain, marketing, and supporting seed production and exports. Potato growers and merchants are still required to register with the Council and it is funded by a levy of approximately £40.00 per hectare for growers and 18 pence per tonne bought by merchants. The acreage grown is checked by aerial survey and compared to growers' returns. Merchants' returns are also checked on a regular basis. It is a criminal offence for growers and merchants not to register and it is a civil offence to submit false returns. Strong partnerships between growers and purchasers result in nearly three-quarters of Britain's current crop being grown on pre-season contracts or for a committed buyer. Nationally, main crop varieties account for almost two-thirds of the area grown and yields have more than doubled from almost twenty-three tonnes per hectare in 1960 to just over forty-seven tonnes per hectare in 2009. This reflects the considerable amount of research, investment and innovation over the years. Modern growers are highly specialised and have good access to the best agronomy and other technical skills, leading to better yields per hectare and a higher quality product for a demanding market. This trend towards highly specialised and capital-intensive businesses is likely to continue, which may lead to even fewer growers, but it is clear that Lincolnshire will remain an extremely important centre for potato production for many years to come.

Chapter 10

THE SUTTON BRIDGE STORY

Charles Parker

Sutton Bridge is in the south east corner of Lincolnshire, on the borders of both Norfolk and Cambridgeshire. At the centre of an extensive potato growing area, it was selected as the location for a research centre, set up by the Potato Marketing Board in 1963.

From its earliest days the Potato Marketing Board had a responsibility to promote and influence research into problems facing the potato industry *(See Chapter 9)*. In 1962 a Research and Development Committee was set up comprised of Board Members and some of the leading agricultural scientists of the day. Among the topics they considered was how to assess and meet the quality requirements of different categories of consumers; how to maintain stable yields to give producers the best financial return with the minimum wastage; and ways of utilising surplus or excess production. This was done in several ways: retail surveys, direct research and development work on farms, public demonstrations of potato machinery, sponsored research through grants to other organisations and institutions, and postgraduate studentship awards for specific research projects.

At that time the main issue facing the industry was how to improve the storage of potatoes. Traditionally, most main crop potatoes were stored on the grower's farm in an earth 'clamp', also known as a 'grave' or 'pie' *(Figure 10.1)*. A shallow, wide trench was dug at the side of the field and lined with straw and the crop was stacked in a long triangular pile on the straw base straight after lifting. The potatoes were covered with thick layers of straw on both sides to protect them from frost and this in turn was covered with the soil taken out of the trench. The straw was left exposed at the top to allow some ventilation. This clamp system did have some problems. If any of the tubers were diseased then this could infect the entire clamp and, depending on the severity of the winter, it was possible for frost or damp to penetrate the covering layer and damage the crop. Clamps could only be opened up when the weather was

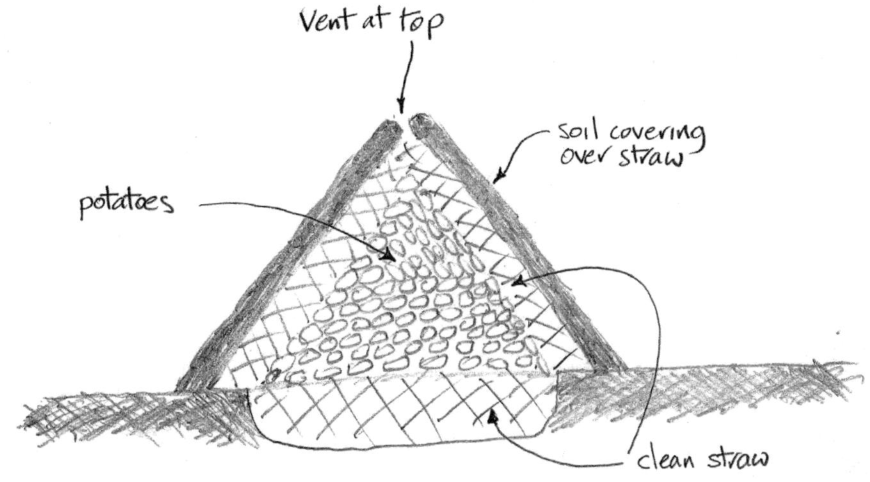

Figure 10.1
A cross section of a potato clamp to show the method of construction. (Charles Parker)

Figure 10.2
Winter at Nocton. Men are removing potatoes from a clamp and bagging them up. They have erected a sacking wind break to provide some protection from a cold wind at this exposed spot.
(Museum of English Rural Life)

favourable and because the crop was bagged or loaded loose onto a cart as it was lifted, this meant that potatoes had to be graded in the open air during the winter. *(Figure 10.2).*

One of the Research and Development Committee's first initiatives was to authorise the investment of about half a million pounds to set up an Experimental Station on a redundant RAF airfield at Sutton Bridge *(Figure 10.3)*. This was to act as a centre for research into all aspects of storing, handling, grading and packing potatoes and to provide specially packed and graded potatoes for trial in industrial and retail markets. The official opening was in October 1964 although the building programme was sufficiently advanced to allow some trial experimental work to be done on the 1963 crop.

There were two distinct sections. The first was a purpose-built potato-grading and pre-packing plant equipped with washing facilities and a dry brushing and grading line. This was equipped and staffed to carry out both experimental and commercial work and it had a large

Figure 10.3
The RAF established their airfield at Sutton Bridge in 1926. This view was taken in the early 1930s. The largest hangar in the lower right is that now occupied by Sutton Bridge Crop Storage Research.
(Courtesy of Terry Hancock)

storage facility which enabled scientific investigations to be carried out alongside the commercial side of the operation. The other section was based in a former RAF hangar *(Figure 10.4)*. It consisted of laboratory scale environmental control cabinets, insulated bin storage units and facilities for testing harvesting and handling machinery. It also carried out investigations into such practical problems as the control of soft rotting in washed, pre-packed potatoes by different peeling methods.

Laboratories and offices were located on the side of the building. In addition, large scale bulk and pallet box stores were built to support the packing plant. Initially, investigations were made into the practical control of environmental conditions within potato stores and the effect of these on the quality of the potatoes after long periods of storage. Other trials led to improvements in the design of clamps, the use of 'Dickie pies' *(Chapter 10.1 & Chapter 11)*. Work was also carried out which led to the introduction of wooden pallet boxes. Particular investigations were made into the curing of potatoes and the use of forced draught through ventilation, humidification and recirculation of artificially chilled air.

Scientific investigations and field trials were carried out in collaboration with the National Agricultural Advisory Service experimental husbandry farms and other research centres, and by the Station staff on the farms of co-operative producers. The effects of different approaches to cultivation and agronomic treatments such as chitting, row widths, chemical weed control and date and method of haulm (top) destruction were investigated. Particular attention was paid to the crop's susceptibility to bruising at harvest time and the amount of damage caused during lifting. Sutton Bridge was the only research station in the country with the facilities to conduct such detailed experimental work and the results were made available to all potato producers with an aim to offer long-term benefit to the entire industry.

Figure 10.4
The interior of the former RAF hangar at Sutton Bridge. Handling equipment and storage crates are in the centre with storage cabinets to either side.
(Courtesy of Graeme Stroud, Potato Council)

In addition to laboratory-based research, the Station produced and test marketed experimental grades for the retail trade. It was at the forefront of the marketing of pre-washed potatoes in polythene bags and it was particularly successful with the introduction of baking potatoes as a retail product in their own right. By careful growing of specific varieties coupled with grading to select consistent sized potatoes with a good skin finish, 'Bakers' evolved from initial trials in 1968/69 to become a key feature of the modern vegetable market. A large number of reports as well as technical papers covering the results of investigations at Sutton Bridge have been published in the farming press and technical journals and talks given at farmers' meetings and conferences.

Both parts of the operation were continuously upgraded to meet changes in the industry. In 1996, in anticipation of the transfer of authority from the Potato Marketing Board to the British Potato Council (BPC), the site was split with the packhouse sold to a commercial operator (now Solanum Ltd.). The BPC subsequently became part of the Agriculture & Horticulture Development Board in 2008 and the research facility was renamed Sutton Bridge Crop Storage Research (SBCSR). A small staff continues to operate out of the old RAF station buildings, the core of which is the 1926 hangar. These facilities have been upgraded and expanded considerably over the last twenty years. In 2010 the Council, in collaboration with the East Midlands Development Agency (EMDA), authorised a further £600,000 investment for a new building specifically for research & training. This will house twenty-four tonnes in bulk bins or sixteen tonnes in boxes and can be configured to operate on refrigeration or ambient air cooling. Virtually any commercial storage configuration

Figure 10.5
Sutton Bridge Crop Storage Research, one of the modern buildings within which some of the experimental cabinets can be seen.
(Courtesy of Graeme Stroud, Potato Council)

can be simulated under controlled scientific conditions *(Figure 10.5)*.

SBCSR is run on a collaborative basis with links to growers, packers, processors and those developing potato handling machinery. Some 60% of the work is directed by the Potato Council, the rest comes from individuals or companies wanting private research, for which they pay. This group includes plant breeders, agrochemical companies and engineering companies working on ventilation, refrigeration, humidity control and loading equipment. There is a wide range of research programmes; about 15-20% is chemistry based, the rest physical/mechanical. Recent work has focussed on trialling new varieties and development of molecular diagnostics (identifying the DNA of the potatoes) *(Figure 10.6)*. They work closely with other research organisations such as the Scottish Crop Research Institute (SCRI), Scottish Agricultural Colleges (SAC) and Cambridge University Farms.

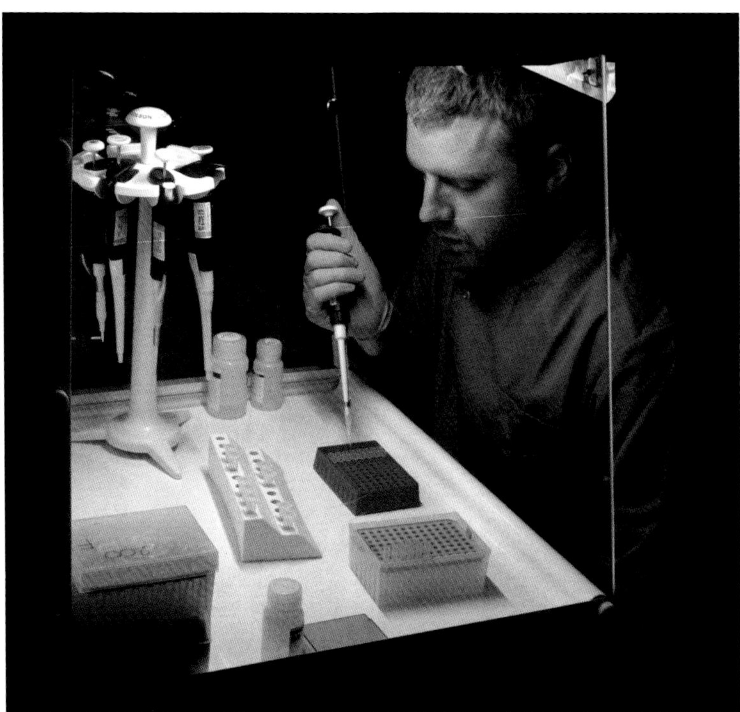

Figure 10.6
At Sutton Bridge, using DNA diagnostics to identify and quantify potato disease.
(Courtesy of Graeme Stroud, Potato Council)

Money to support the site comes from levy on all growers and those who trade in potatoes; it is not taxpayer funded. The main purpose of SBCSR's research remains the maintenance of the quality of stored potatoes for different uses over a period of about nine months (i.e. until the next season's potatoes are ready for lifting). Since the facility first opened, the potato industry has consolidated, with significantly fewer growers who have become increasingly professional and scientific in their approach. The market for processed potatoes has become increasingly important and it now accounts for more than 50% of potato trade. Yields have increased significantly over the last fifty years but that is now levelling off and the current emphasis is on lower inputs – cutting costs, maximising returns and minimising energy use. This has required significant capital investment in machinery and controlled storage is an essential part of this.

A key part of the development of improved storage has been the use of suppressants which prevent new sprouts starting to grow while the tubers are in store as this leads to weight loss and deterioration in quality. Chemical suppressants come in gaseous, liquid and granular form and their use has to be very carefully monitored. SBCSR personnel have developed the expertise to handle most of the latest equipment for chemical application, ranging from granule applicators to hydraulic and electrostatic sprayers. These are used as the crop is going into store; alternatively, buildings can be treated by 'hot fogging' which utilises machinery to warm the suppressant and vapourise it so that it can be distributed evenly over the crop when it is already in store.

SBCSR have also forged collaborative links to other centres with expertise in application technology and analysis of residual traces of chemicals in the potato tubers when they come out of store (from fertilisers and sprout suppressants). The appearance of potatoes coming out of store is important as attractive samples will yield higher prices than those stored in poorer conditions. Cooking tests are carried out both on samples purchased and on potatoes involved in the various experiments and storage investigations.

Whole potatoes for pre-pack can be stored at 3°C while potatoes for processing need 7-10°C; this is achieved by the control of temperature, humidity, ventilation and preventing sprout growth. Fry testing is done for chips/crisps for twelve to fifteen weeks each year. Fry colour (which depends on the sugar content of the tubers) is most important for chips and crisps and tests are conducted both going into store and coming out of store to monitor changes.

Only small amounts of potatoes are needed to carry out this work; 300 tonnes is the maximum that can be stored but normally about 150 tonnes are held in four different sizes of controlled environment store (3 tonne, 6 tonne, 12 tonne and 24 tonne). In addition there are fourteen Controlled Atmosphere cabinets capable of maintaining modified oxygen and carbon dioxide conditions within the fully controlled temperature regimes of the controlled environment rooms. These small scale cabinets allow detailed investigations to be undertaken using a wide range of atmospheric conditions. Extreme atmospheres can be generated within hours and maintained over long periods. Each room is able to operate between 2°C and 20°C and between 80% and 98% relative humidity. Other storage conditions can be simulated on request. Monitoring and control are by computerised systems to close tolerances.

The Sutton Bridge staff has a pool of expertise that does not exist elsewhere and they provide advisory services on an individual basis to growers and processors throughout Britain. This demand is growing and becoming global; in recent years services have been provided to organisations in the United States of America and Japan. The Council's objectives for the facility are to ensure that it is a cost-effective research centre working for the benefit of the British potato industry. To achieve this, it has to bid for levy-funded research contracts and undertake a wide range of technology transfer activities. It is also free to acquire external, private business. As part of this obligation, SBCSR provides free initial advice and information to levy payers. A key aim is to integrate storage work at SBCSR into the whole spectrum of science in support of the potato industry. The future looks positive for Sutton Bridge; however it may have to become a fully funded independent research organisation if the compulsory Potato Council levy is ever removed.

10.1 POTATO STORAGE

Cathérine Wilson

New potatoes are those that are harvested at a small size before maturity. They do not store well and so are sold straight after harvesting. They command a premium price but the yields are lower so the profit margin for the grower is not necessarily larger.

Main crop potatoes or *Ware* are generally harvested from the end of September through October, and are then stored in some way so that they keep in good condition for as long as possible.

The traditional way of keeping the harvested crop was to pile them into a mound at the edge of the field or other convenient location. They were stored straight from the field without any cleaning or grading. The pile, which was as long as was necessary to accommodate the crop, was then covered with straw and sometimes soil to protect the contents against frost. These piles were known as clamps, graves or pies depending on local custom. When the potatoes were needed the pile was opened; the potatoes were put through a hand riddle to remove stones, surplus soil, and 'smalls'*(Figure 10.1.1)*; and the potatoes were put into hessian sacks for transport to wherever they were needed. This practice meant that the potatoes only had to be moved once, but the riddling, or later grading through a portable grader, had to be done out of doors often in the depths of winter. As clamps could only be opened up when the weather was favourable access to this important food source could be restricted in extended periods of bad weather.

Whilst clamping did preserve the crop to some extent it was often found that the potatoes in the middle had become damp and gone rotten, due to lack of ventilation; or one bad potato, put into the pie without being noticed, could infect others around it, leading to significant losses. Also in years of heavy frost the straw covering may not prove adequate to prevent damage. One of the main roles of the Sutton Bridge Experimental Station when it was set up in 1963 was to carry out experiments to reduce the significant wastage which resulted from this method of storage *(see Chapter 10.)*

Figure 10.1.1
Hand riddling at Old Leake, left to right: Roger Fixter, George White, 'Grandad' White, Jack White.
(Courtesy of the White family, Old Leake)

One early experiment was to install a ventilation duct at ground level underneath the pie and cover the pie with soil as well as straw *(Figure 10.1.2)*.

An improved version of the pie was introduced on to some farms. Where the pie was to be built a slatted ventilation duct was installed. Straw bales were placed on top of one another to form two parallel 'walls' about twelve feet apart on either side of this duct, sometimes with polythene sheeting placed vertically between the bales. The potatoes were then tipped in between these 'walls' and the pie topped off with straw and more polythene. These temporary structures were known as Dickie pies, after a Mr Dickie of Holbeach who first developed the idea. [1]

The idea was then taken further, at least on Worth Farms, where 'permanent' Dickie pies were built. The straw bale walls were replaced by concrete walls about

Figure 10.1.2
Air duct beneath clamp of King Edwards to provide natural convection.
(Courtesy of Nick Twell, Sutton Bridge)

twelve feet apart and up to 100 feet long. They held 250 tons of potatoes when full. They had a ventilation duct dug below ground level, so the base on which the potatoes were put was flat. Vertical ventilation ducts were also installed and when the pie was full these were capped off with small covered 'chimneys' which could be opened or closed to provide some regulation to the temperature and humidity in the pie. These structures were quite effective and were used alongside storage in buildings into the 1990s *(Figure 10.1.3). (See Chapter 11)*

However, storage in a building reduced some of the difficulties and uncertainties of outdoor storage and particularly reduced risks of damage and rot. As early as 1954 the then Ministry of Agriculture and Fisheries published an advisory booklet on *Bulk Storage of Potatoes in Buildings.* Storage in buildings gave independence from the weather, better working conditions and reduced losses from disease due to the drier conditions. It also saved time as access to the potatoes was easier and they could be graded and bagged in advance of requirements.[2] The leaflet gives detailed advice on the recommended size and shape for new buildings; on how to adapt old buildings; on insulation and ventilation to achieve best results, but points out the disadvantage of the initial capital expenditure needed. The stack of potatoes should still be covered with straw to prevent greening and to absorb moisture from the potatoes.

At this date the potatoes were simply transported from the field and piled in the building with no temperature control. This was known as *bulk storage* in an *ambient* store.

With the development of forklifts which could be fitted on to tractors, and the introduction of mechanical handlers on farms, it became possible to transport potatoes in large crates, rather than loose. From the 1960s one-ton crates were introduced and are now standard. Most potatoes now go straight into crates (boxes) as they are harvested and the crates go into store until needed. Some stores are temperature controlled but for cost and environmental reasons, the emphasis now is on constructing well insulated and ventilated buildings which will maintain appropriate conditions without the need for additional temperature control.

Whilst some growers have their own purpose built stores, others use facilities provided by specialists in this field. Charles Porter of Stamford, a potato merchant, pioneered large scale potato storage in the early 1970s on a site at Honeypot Lane, South Witham. He started by storing 5-10,000 tons but expanded the

Figure 10.1.3
Dickie pie using straw bales at Sutton Bridge *(Courtesy of Nick Twell, Sutton Bridge)*

business significantly over the years and by 1990 was storing 95,000 tons, mainly for McCains and Walkers Crisps. It was the largest potato storage complex in the UK at that time. The business, now known as C E P (Charles Edward Porter) Potatoes, is still operating from the same site and comprises buildings for both bulk and box storage, all temperature controlled.[3]

Potatoes can now be stored year round if kept in suitable stores but need to be treated with Chloroisophenyl carbonate (CIPC) to prevent early chitting. Key trials for this treatment were carried out at Chris Howard's cold store at Nocton where potatoes were successfully stored until June. Trials were also carried out at Bentley Nelstrop's farm at Westfield, Bracebridge Heath. These trials, which began in the 1960s, helped the development of CIPC, a treatment which continues to be used today; and continual improvements are researched at Sutton Bridge. Year-round storage has had a considerable impact on the UK potato industry. For example in the 1960s Golden Wonder crisps were importing potatoes from Cyprus for part of the year, for their Corby factory. By using CIPC they were able to use British potatoes through the year. The annual factory costs reduced by £25,000 and local farmers benefited by the extra production value of their potatoes.[4]

In storage, as in so many other aspects of potato growing, Lincolnshire has played, and continues to play, a significant role.

Endnotes

1 Peter Shepherd, *pers. com.*

2 *Bulk Storage of Potatoes in Buildings,* Ministry of Agriculture and Fisheries, Leaflet No. 24, 1954, HMSO

3 Richard Harris, *pers. com.*

4 Richard Harris, *pers. com.*

Chapter 11

GROWING AND SELLING POTATOES, 1960-2010

Catherine Wilson

The world of potato growing and marketing today is dramatically different to the situation in the 1960s. There has been a continuous process of improvement in growing and harvesting techniques; in scientific approaches to pest and disease control; and in vastly better storage to ensure that potatoes can be supplied in good condition for twelve months of the year. But the potato business in Lincolnshire is no longer just about growing: a significant part of the packing, processing, marketing and distribution of potatoes to most of the major supermarkets also takes place in Lincolnshire and keeps many local people in work.

This is an increasingly sophisticated and competitive business to which growers and suppliers have to respond in order to retain their market share. Innovation and flexibility in our potato industry not only continue to put potatoes on our plates but do so in ways that are convenient for today's time-poor consumers. In this chapter we explore these changes through the eyes of some of those who make their livelihoods in this industry which is still so important to the county.

In 1960 there were 76,825 registered potato growers in the UK cultivating 280,000 hectares at an average of 33.65 hectares per grower. The net yield was 22.8 tonnes per hectare. By 1980 there were 30,225 growers growing an average of 5.76 hectares with a yield of 37.2 tonnes per hectare. After another twenty years, by 2000, there were only 6143 growers cultivating an average of 21.80 hectares producing 41 tonnes per hectare. This trend has continued so that in 2009 there were only 2609 growers but they were cultivating an average of 47.37 hectares each with a yield of 47.6 tonnes per hectare.[1] Of these 2609 growers, 374 are in Lincolnshire and together they grow some 13,900 hectares.[2] This is the largest area of any county, and is significantly larger than the nearest 'rivals', Cambridgeshire and Norfolk.

The dramatic decrease in the number of people involved in growing potatoes has been driven by the increasingly specialised nature of the business. The very significant increase in yields has been made possible by a more scientific approach to controlling pests and diseases, increasing use of fertilisers, and particularly by irrigation where this is possible.

Over the same period the pattern of potato consumption has undergone equally dramatic changes. In the 1960s the general picture was that potatoes were sold whole, unwashed, in 56lb bags from the farm door or, mainly, through wholesalers. The consumer bought the whole potatoes, took them home, washed and peeled them and then boiled, mashed or roasted them according to taste. Potatoes remain a major part of the British diet, though the average yearly consumption for each person has declined slightly from 108 kilograms in 1988 to 90 kg in 2009. But of this quantity only 42.8 kg are now eaten fresh, a decrease from 72 kg in 1988. The rest are eaten as processed potatoes, in prepared meals or as frozen chips, crisps and other snacks.[3] Also, although potatoes remain a major part of the UK diet, the percentage of rice, pasta and other carbohydrates consumed is increasing so that the potato needs to compete for convenience to retain its popularity with the British consumer *(Figure 11.1).*

The major producers have needed to respond to these changes. As well as specialist packing of raw potatoes for each different customer, supermarkets now require a variety of prepared products that are ready to cook either in the oven or the microwave cooker without peeling or other preparation. Our consumption of frozen and chilled potato products now equals the consumption of raw potatoes[4] *(Figure 11.2)*. In addition, there have, for many years, been specialist food processing companies in the county: the crisp manufacturers mentioned in Chapter 7 and such companies as PAS at Easton, near Grantham, described in Chapter 8. The variety of prepared foods continues to increase, emphasising the versatile nature of the potato: spicy wedges, hash browns, curly fries are all now on the menu to encourage us to keep eating potatoes.

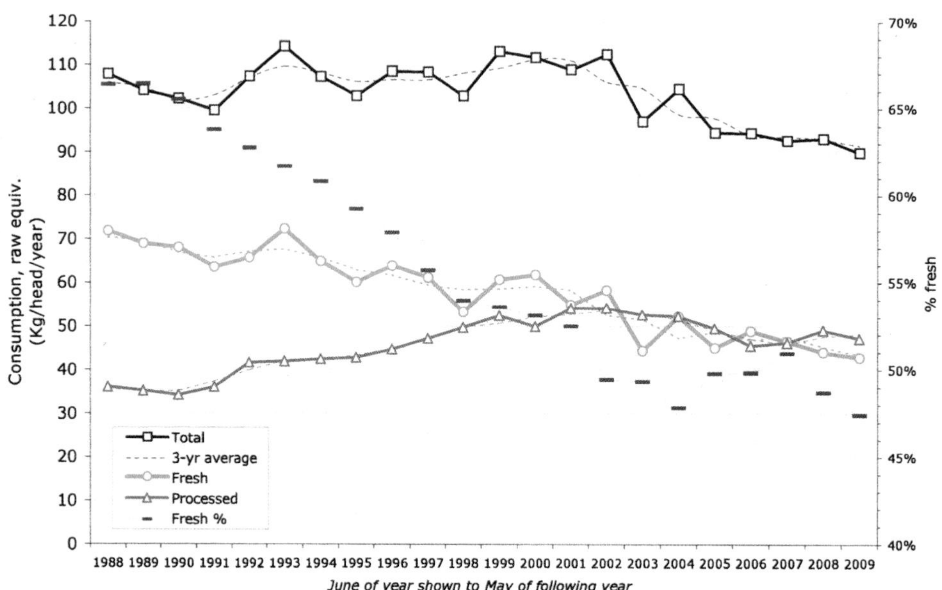

Figure 11.1
Per capita consumption of potatoes in GB 1988-2009. (Potato Council)

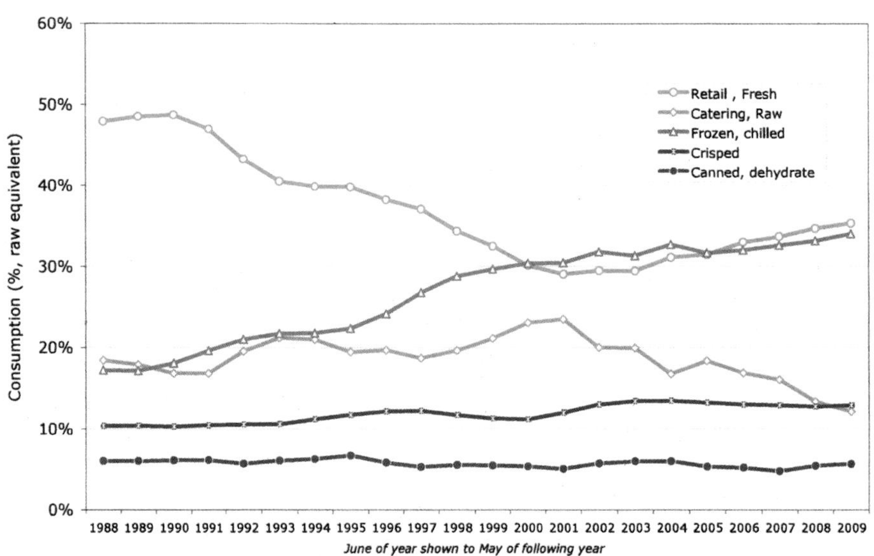

Figure 11.2
Consumption by product groups 1988-2009. (Potato Council)

Lincolnshire has several major growers and farming cooperatives which grow on contract for particular supermarkets. The quantity and varieties grown are dictated by the needs of the supermarkets, which require year-round quality and a constant reliable supply. There are also smaller-scale growers providing potatoes for direct sale through farm shops and farmers' markets and through the wholesalers who in turn supply the catering trade and street markets countrywide.

Since the Potato Marketing Board was replaced by the British Potato Council in 1997, there are no quotas for potatoes, so each farmer can decide how many hectares to grow on an annual basis. The picture across the county is infinitely variable, and we can only give a snapshot here but the following series of case studies will indicate how the system has developed over the last 50 years and how it works now.

David Armstrong *(Figure 11.3)* farms a total of 1400 acres in and around Bardney. His father came from Scotland in 1957 and at that time grew about 6 hectares of potatoes. David took over the potato side of the business in 1990 and now grows about 65 hectares, but winter wheat is his main cash crop and he also grows peas, beet, linseed and rape. The Potato Cyst Nematode (PCN), or eelworm, is a pest which can remain active in the soil for eight to ten years so potatoes can only be grown on a long rotation if the use of expensive

Figure 11.3
David Armstrong (centre) with James Robertson & David Nelson from Branston.
(Courtesy of Andy Weekes, Branston Ltd.)

Figure 11.4
Irrigation equipment on site.
(Courtesy of Andy Weekes, via Branston Ltd.)

and unpleasant pesticides is to be avoided. PCN is a particular problem in the easily cultivated soils of the Fens. David's own land, which is mainly fen edge soils, is therefore only used for potatoes a minimum of every eight years. Other land is rented on an annual basis from farmers within about a five mile radius of Bardney. There is no fixed arrangement as the amount and location of land rented changes every year, so it is dependent on good relationships with neighbours.

The annual yield is about fifty tonnes per hectare. Yields have increased significantly over recent years due to improvements in varieties, but also due to irrigation which he believes is now an essential feature of a successful potato crop. David uses water from the River Witham and its tributaries for this purpose, using mobile irrigation equipment *(Figure 11.4)*. The quality of water to be used has to be approved by the Crop Assurance Scheme to ensure it is suitable for use on food crops. The Environment Agency agrees the amount of water that can be abstracted and issues a licence which has to be paid for. This, to some extent, dictates where he can rent land as it has to be close enough to an approved water course for his irrigation equipment to work.

David has large temperature-controlled stores at his farm where the harvested crop is stored in standard one-tonne crates until it is required *(Figure 11.5)*. This has also required significant investment, but is necessary to keep the crop in good condition. Potato 'pies' in fields are no longer acceptable!

Figure 11.5
David Armstrong's temperature controlled stores and storage crates. (Catherine Wilson)

His main contract is with Branston Ltd. who supply Tesco – he currently supplies 700 tonnes annually to them. He also grows 500 tonnes on contract for Greenvale, a large distribution group with a processing plant at March, Cambs. This contracted tonnage represents 40% of David's total. The other 60 % is 'free buy', sold sometimes to Branston and Greenvale but also on the open market, dependent on the price and state of the market. This gives flexibility but it is not risk free. The price of 'free buy' can vary between £50 and £300 per tonne. When to sell the stored potatoes depends on his 'gut feeling' about the market using his years of experience, and can also depend on cash flow. He tends to sell his 'free buy' crop in smaller units, perhaps 25 tonnes at a time.

David's aim is to produce a quality end product for which he can get the best price. The big supermarkets do assessment audits of the farm and the crop to ensure they are to the required standard. There also needs to be complete traceability, so every application of pesticide, herbicide and fertiliser has to be recorded for each field. There is a great deal of paperwork involved. David is a member of the Branston producer group and uses the services of an agronomist from Branston for specialist advice such as when to spray for blight or when to stop growth in the autumn.

If some of the uncertainty of growing potatoes has been reduced by a more scientific approach, it has been replaced to some extent by uncertainty about when to sell and who to sell to. However David feels this is better than the quota system under the Potato Marketing Board. He has put significant investment into building temperature controlled stores on his farm, into irrigation equipment and into the latest machinery to get maximum return from his acreage. He needs to be able to grow the area and tonnage necessary to justify that investment and to fulfil the market requirements.

A different, more traditional, approach is still practised on some smaller farms. **The Daubney family** of Old Leake have been farming land there since Henry Daubney moved from Wyberton and bought 18 acres of good silt land in 1908. The farm is now about sixty hectares (150 acres) and is farmed by Henry's grandson, Frank Henry, and his two sons Alan and John. It is a mixed farm with some cattle and grazing land, growing wheat and a variety of vegetable crops. They have always grown potatoes but the amount varies from as low as around three hectares up to ten to twelve hectares. They are completely independent and are not involved with any supermarkets. They make their own decisions on a year by year basis about what, and how much, to grow. The amount of potato acreage will depend on the rotation of other crops, market predictions and other factors. Unlike

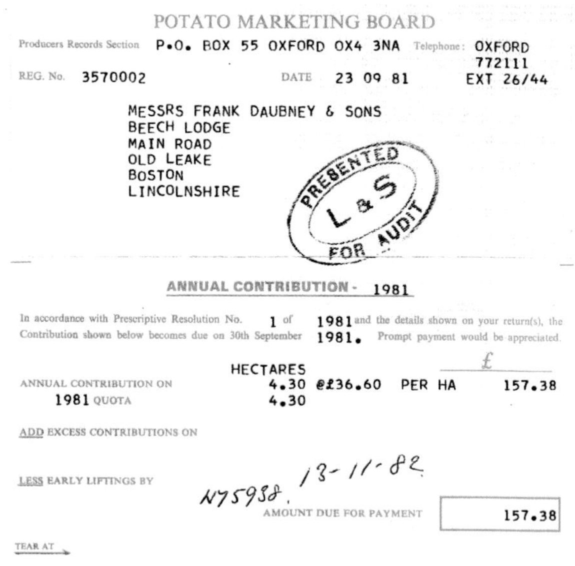

POTATO MARKETING BOARD

Producers Records Section P.O. BOX 55 OXFORD OX4 3NA Telephone: OXFORD 772111 EXT 26/44

REG. No. 3570002 DATE 23 09 81

MESSRS FRANK DAUBNEY & SONS
BEECH LODGE
MAIN ROAD
OLD LEAKE
BOSTON
LINCOLNSHIRE

PRESENTED L & S FOR AUDIT

ANNUAL CONTRIBUTION - 1981

In accordance with Prescriptive Resolution No. 1 of 1981 and the details shown on your return(s), the Contribution shown below becomes due on 30th September 1981. Prompt payment would be appreciated.

	HECTARES		£
ANNUAL CONTRIBUTION ON	4.30	@£36.60 PER HA	157.38
1981 QUOTA	4.30		

ADD EXCESS CONTRIBUTIONS ON

LESS EARLY LIFTINGS BY

N75938. 13-11-82

AMOUNT DUE FOR PAYMENT 157.38

TEAR AT

Figure 11.6
Receipt for hectarage payment to Potato Marketing Board, 1981. (Courtesy of F. Daubney)

David Armstrong they use only their own land but it is less susceptible to PCN (eelworm) so it can be used for potatoes every four or five years, rather than the longer rotation necessary on the damper fen soils. They are a Registered Grower and make an annual payment to the Potato Marketing Board/Potato Council depending on the acreage grown *(Figure 11.6).*

They buy seed potato, via a merchant, usually from Scotland but sometimes from Ireland *(Figure 11.7).* This seed is planted one year and grown on but not to full size as it is then harvested for seed for the next year. One tonne purchased can become fifteen tonnes for seed the following year whilst retaining the disease resistant properties of the original seed. The aim is to get seed of near equal size to make planting easier. But a balance is needed. The smaller the seed, the more potatoes to the tonne, but if they are too small the productivity is reduced. Graded seed is planted at one tonne to the acre. The Daubneys have all their own equipment and do not use contractors.

760 kilograms of fertiliser are put on the soil before planting for a ware crop but only half that rate for a seed crop *(Figure 11.8).* No other fertiliser is used. They do not use an agronomist but seek advice if needed from the company supplying the chemicals.

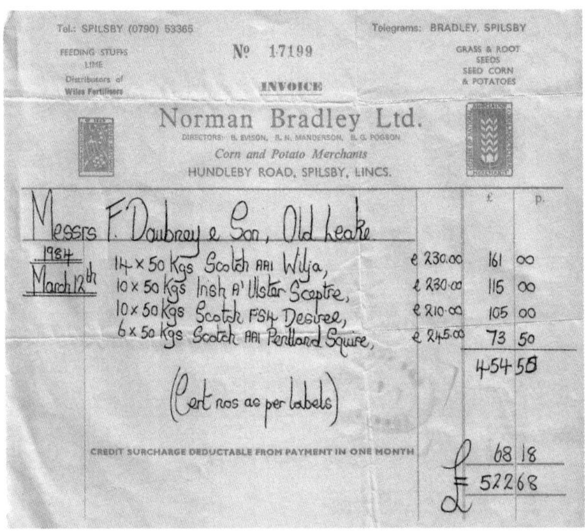

Tel.: SPILSBY (0790) 53365 — Telegrams: BRADLEY, SPILSBY

FEEDING STUFFS
LIME
Distributors of
Wiles Fertilisers

№ 17199

INVOICE

GRASS & ROOT
SEEDS
SEED CORN
& POTATOES

Norman Bradley Ltd.
DIRECTORS: B. EVISON, R. N. MANDERSON, B. G. POGSON
Corn and Potato Merchants
HUNDLEBY ROAD, SPILSBY, LINCS.

Messrs F. Daubney & Son, Old Leake

			£	p.
1984 March 12th	14 x 50 Kgs Scotch AA1 Wilja,	@ 230.00	161	00
	10 x 50 Kgs Irish A1 Ulster Sceptre,	@ 230.00	115	00
	10 x 50 Kgs Scotch FS4 Desiree,	@ 210.00	105	00
	6 x 50 Kgs Scotch AA1 Pentland Squire,	@ 245.00	73	50
			454	50
	(Cert nos as per labels)			
	CREDIT SURCHARGE DEDUCTABLE FROM PAYMENT IN ONE MONTH		68	18
		£	522	68

Figure 11.7
Invoice for Scottish & Irish seed potatoes, 1984.
(Courtesy of F. Daubney)

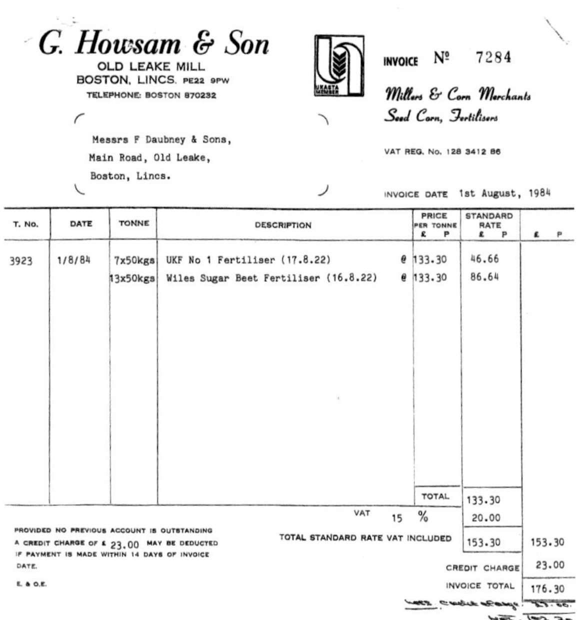

G. Howsam & Son
OLD LEAKE MILL
BOSTON, LINCS. PE22 9PW
TELEPHONE: BOSTON 870232

INVOICE № 7284
Millers & Corn Merchants
Seed Corn, Fertilisers

Messrs F Daubney & Sons,
Main Road, Old Leake,
Boston, Lincs.

VAT REG. No. 128 3412 86

INVOICE DATE 1st August, 1984

T. No.	DATE	TONNE	DESCRIPTION	PRICE PER TONNE £ P	STANDARD RATE £ P	£ P
3923	1/8/84	7x50kgs	UKF No 1 Fertiliser (17.8.22) @	133.30	46.66	
		13x50kgs	Wiles Sugar Beet Fertiliser (16.8.22) @	133.30	86.64	
				TOTAL	133.30	
			VAT 15 %		20.00	
			TOTAL STANDARD RATE VAT INCLUDED		153.30	153.30
					CREDIT CHARGE	23.00
					INVOICE TOTAL	176.30

PROVIDED NO PREVIOUS ACCOUNT IS OUTSTANDING A CREDIT CHARGE OF £ 23.00 MAY BE DEDUCTED IF PAYMENT IS MADE WITHIN 14 DAYS OF INVOICE DATE.

E. & O.E.

Figure 11.8
Invoice for purchase of fertiliser, 1984.
(Courtesy of F. Daubney)

Chemicals used include a foliage feed, a herbicide to reduce weed growth, and a spray against blight but only when needed. The crop is not irrigated but relies on natural rainfall. This reduces costs, and though yields are lower the costs balance out. The haulm is killed off with a desiccant in September; the potatoes are left in the ground for a few weeks for the skins to set and then lifted in late September or early October. Some years they grow 'new' potatoes which are not stored but sold immediately at a premium price. If these are left in the ground longer they become 'early' potatoes but they still need to be sold without storing and attract a higher price than the main 'ware' crop. The yields are considerably lower, perhaps seven and a half tonnes per hectare for 'new' and twenty tonnes per hectare for 'early' as opposed to thirty-seven tonnes per hectare or more for ware, but the price difference makes it worthwhile.

The ware goes straight into ambient temperature stores in boxes or in bulk. They do not have refrigerated storage as it is costly to install and run. The potatoes keep well but not as long as they would in a temperature controlled store. When ready for sale the potatoes are

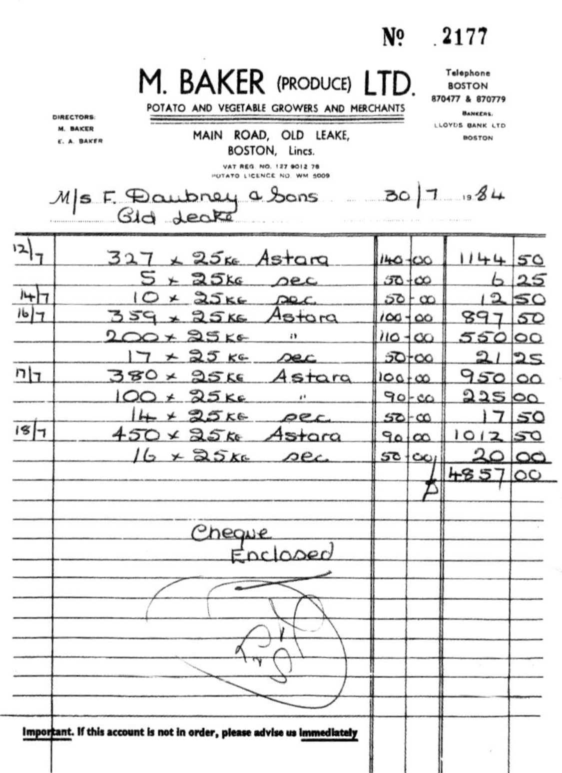

№ 2177

M. BAKER (PRODUCE) LTD.

POTATO AND VEGETABLE GROWERS AND MERCHANTS

DIRECTORS: M. BAKER, E. A. BAKER

MAIN ROAD, OLD LEAKE, BOSTON, Lincs.

VAT REG. NO. 127 9012 78
POTATO LICENCE NO. WM 5009

Telephone BOSTON 870477 & 870779

BANKERS: LLOYDS BANK LTD BOSTON

M/s F. Daubney & Sons 30/7 1984
Old Leake

12/7	327 × 25KG Astara	140·00	1144 50
	5 × 25KG sec	50·00	6 25
14/7	10 × 25KG sec	50·00	12 50
16/7	359 × 25KG Astara	100·00	897 50
	200 × 25KG "	110·00	550 00
	17 × 25 KG sec	50·00	21 25
17/7	380 × 25KG Astara	100·00	950 00
	100 × 25KG "	90·00	225 00
	14 × 25KG sec	50·00	17 50
18/7	450 × 25KG Astara	90·00	1012 50
	16 × 25KG sec	50·00	20 00
		£	4857 00

Cheque Enclosed

Important. If this account is not in order, please advise us immediately

Figure 11.9
Receipt for purchase of potatoes, 1984.
(Courtesy of F. Daubney)

graded and brushed on the farm, then packed into twenty-five kilogram paper sacks and sold through merchants to the wholesale market *(Figure 11.9)*. The Daubneys pay haulage to get the crop to the wholesale market at £40 per tonne, and also pay for the paper sacks *(Figure 11.10)*. From the wholesalers the crop goes to the regular street markets and the catering trade. The potatoes are sold 'on commission'. The merchant gets the best price he can, then retains a percentage for himself. It is in the merchant's interests to get the best price possible but there is no guaranteed price to the grower until they have been sold. The Daubneys decide the best time to sell depending on the state of the market, the cost of storage, the quality of crop, cash-flow needs and their own workload.

Another fourth generation farming family operates on a rather different scale.

A. H. Worth & Co. Ltd., the family business established by Arthur Hovenden Worth, *(see Chapter 3)* still has a significant involvement with potato growing and is increasingly involved with packing and processing from its headquarters at Holbeach Hurn. **Tony Worth**, A. H. Worth's grandson, went to Australia as a young man to gain experience but returned to join the family business in 1968. He led the company through thirty years of innovation, development and expansion until he passed the baton on to his son Duncan who is now the Managing Director, and a member of the Potato Council. Tony Worth is now the Lord Lieutenant of Lincolnshire.

Peter Shepherd started work, at the age of eighteen, as a farm apprentice at Worth Farms in 1950, the first farm apprentice they had had. So he has experienced at first hand many of the changes that have taken place in the last sixty years, and indeed was at the cutting edge of some of them.

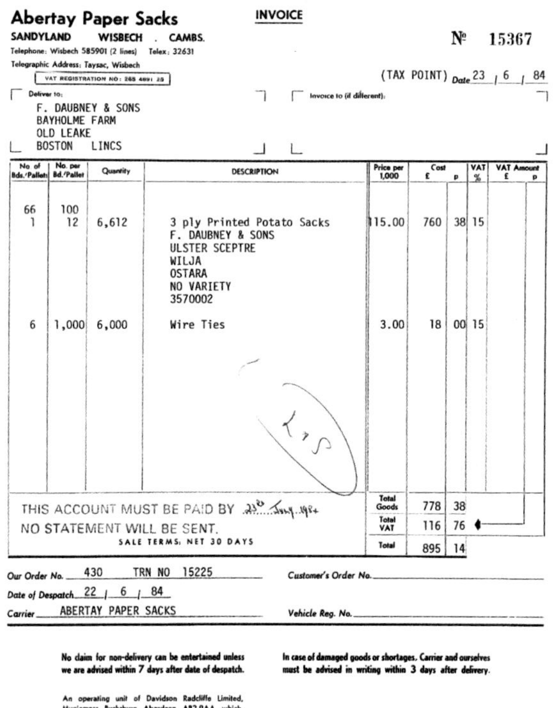

Abertay Paper Sacks INVOICE

SANDYLAND WISBECH . CAMBS.

Telephone: Wisbech 585901 (2 lines) Telex: 32631

Telegraphic Address: Taysac, Wisbech

VAT REGISTRATION NO: 265 4891 25

№ 15367

(TAX POINT) Date 23 / 6 / 84

Deliver to:
F. DAUBNEY & SONS
BAYHOLME FARM
OLD LEAKE
BOSTON LINCS

Invoice to (if different):

No. of Bds./Pallets	No. per Bd./Pallet	Quantity	DESCRIPTION	Price per 1,000	Cost £	p	VAT %	VAT Amount £	p
66 1	100 12	6,612	3 ply Printed Potato Sacks F. DAUBNEY & SONS ULSTER SCEPTRE WILJA OSTARA NO VARIETY 3570002	115.00	760	38	15		
6	1,000	6,000	Wire Ties	3.00	18	00	15		
			Total Goods		778	38			
			Total VAT		116	76			
			Total		895	14			

THIS ACCOUNT MUST BE PAID BY 23rd July 1984
NO STATEMENT WILL BE SENT.
SALE TERMS: NET 30 DAYS

Our Order No. 430 TRN NO 15225 Customer's Order No.

Date of Despatch 22 / 6 / 84

Carrier ABERTAY PAPER SACKS Vehicle Reg. No.

No claim for non-delivery can be entertained unless we are advised within 7 days after date of despatch.

In case of damaged goods or shortages, Carrier and ourselves must be advised in writing within 3 days after delivery.

An operating unit of Davidson Radcliffe Limited, Mugiemoss, Bucksburn, Aberdeen, AB2 9AA, which is a member of the BPB Industries Group of Companies.

Figure 11.10
Invoice for purchase of paper sacks, 1984.
(Courtesy of F. Daubney)

He has written a detailed account of his first eighteen months' work and his experiences must be typical of many farms at that time. They were using tractors, but alongside horses and what machinery there was did not cut out much of the back-breaking work. He records that one of his first jobs was to harrow the potato ridges with horse drawn harrows. For this purpose a single Suffolk Punch horse (called Rattler) was used. Peter had not worked horses before. The tradition in south Lincolnshire and the Fens generally was for the horse to be driven using one rein only, not two, and to direct the horse by voice command, using a broad south Lincolnshire dialect otherwise the horse would not understand. All went well on the straight with Rattler pulling four harrows on top of four potato ridges, but at the end of the field Peter turned the horse too tightly with the result that the harrow pole stuck in the ground, the harrows up-ended and landed on Rattler's back, who promptly (and unsurprisingly) bolted![5]

Another potato related task was spraying the crop against potato blight in June. As Peter records:

> A. H. Worth was one of the early pioneers of intensive potato growing in South Lincolnshire and one of the challenges that he had to overcome was the control of blight. He introduced a Bordeaux mixture of fine powder (mainly copper) and invented a machine to apply this mixture to the potato crop. The machine was horse-drawn and had a small hopper which contained the powder. A chain in the bottom of the hopper fed the powder into a fan chamber which blew the mixture into metal tubes with spouts that were centred over each of the nine potato rows. The chain and fan were driven by the land wheels of the sprayer, which was called a Gratton after the local agricultural machinery merchant who manufactured it to A. H. Worth's patent.[6] *(Grattons of Boston, see Chapter 5)*

October was the time for harvesting the main crop potatoes; a typical gang comprised eight men picking, one man 'graving', a tractor man ploughing or hoovering-out, and three horses and carts and two drivers. At that time main crop potatoes were stored in clamps.

Peter was also involved with carting the seed potatoes out from the glasshouses to the fields for planting, using the then still operative farm railway *(see Panel 5.1)*; and then joining the potato planting gang. There were three men to a chitting tray, two of whom carried the tray and planted a row each, with the third man walking behind and planting the middle row. And then there was the task of riddling last year's potatoes out of the graves, first clearing the soil and straw that had been placed on top, then forking the potatoes into the 'rocker' or riddling machine, picking out the rotten or damaged potatoes by hand and loading them into eight stone (one cwt or the equivalent of fifty-one kilograms) hessian sacks for transport to the markets.

Most of the work on the farm at that time was piece-work, paid by the acres worked or the number of bags riddled so it was continuous hard work.

After his eighteen months as an apprentice, Peter went to Caythorpe Agricultural College, little knowing that after his training he would be invited back to become Foreman of the Whitehouse Lodge Farm where he had served his apprenticeship. He remained with Worth Farms for the rest of his career, retiring as Manager of the farming operation in 1989.

In the 1950s Worth Farms operated three farms which were run fairly independently, each with its own foreman and workforce. Peter's responsibilities included 600 acres with thirty men and a female gang for planting and picking. But by 1965 the farms were brought together and Peter became Estate Manager for all 2000 acres.

He introduced an early example of an indoor grading line in the late 1960s when the QV brand was introduced (QV was decided on as a name after Dick Worth, the then head of the company, looked up the word 'worth' in a thesaurus. Two of the synonyms were quality and value, hence QV). In the late 1960s all potatoes were packed in 56lb sacks for sale mainly to the London market. Dick Worth wanted his potatoes to be distinctive for quality. By branding them with the logo, customers would get to know the quality and come back for more.

Figure 11.11
Early electronic defect recognition system.
(Courtesy of P. Shepherd)

Figure 11.12a
Multi-row harvesting with a prototype machine made by Johnsons of March in the 1960s. Digger with right-hand delivery. (Courtesy of P. Shepherd)

Figure 11.12b
Digger with left-hand delivery.
(Courtesy of P. Shepherd)

Holbeach Marsh Co-operative was formed in 1968 when a group of local farmers got together for joint marketing, initially of peas and other frozen vegetables which were just becoming popular. They also marketed potatoes, with Worths as the managing agents, a situation that continued until 1993 when A. H. Worth & Co. Ltd. bought the potato side of the business from the other members of the co-operative.

In the 1970s Peter Shepherd worked with Essex University to develop a system of electronic grading of potatoes, an early attempt to detect, optically, green or damaged potatoes *(Figure 11.11)*. However, it was not very successful as the technology was not sufficiently developed at that time.

In the 1960s Worth Farms started using Johnson single row potato harvesters, the first real mechanisation of the harvesting process. This was followed by trying a six-row windrow approach with a machine lifting two rows and delivering them into the middle of a third row which were then all lifted together into trailers *(Figure 11-12 a-d)*. This speeded up the harvesting but left the potatoes exposed to the weather if it rained suddenly, and the transport and storage then in place were inadequate to cope with the speed of the harvest. Undercover storage in sheds was beginning to replace the clamps in the fields but an interim, and cheaper, method was to use 'Dickie pies'. These were an improved version of the freestanding clamp or pie and consisted of a long rectangular area with walls of either straw bales or, later, concrete with two channels running along the length at ground level with slats for ventilation. The potatoes were put between these walls, then covered with straw and a layer of polythene, then more straw. At regular intervals along the top air vents were located which could be opened or closed to provide some degree of temperature and humidity control *(Figures 11.13 & 11.14)*. Dickie pies were in use until the early 1990s (see Chapter 10.1).

Developing a mechanical harvester for potatoes is not as straightforward as it is for grain crops, as fresh potatoes

Figure 11.12c
Digger with straight through delivery.
(Courtesy of P. Shepherd)

Gary Naylor was born in Holbeach and apart from three months in Canada has stayed in the area all his life. Having trained in farm management he joined the Worth Company as trainee farm manager in 1984; he became farms manager in 1989 and still works for the company, now as Farms Director and is responsible for the farming operation. In 1984 the farm was still 2000 acres, of which 200 acres were growing potatoes and eighteen men were employed. The yield was about 20 tons per acre, all of which was sold through the Holbeach Marsh Co-operative.

Trailed harvesters were used then, only being replaced by the self-propelled machines in 2004. There was one store which could take 450 standard one-tonne boxes

Figure 11.12d
The windrowed potatoes being lifted into a trailer.
(Courtesy of P. Shepherd)

Figure 11.13
The start of a Dickie Pie with straw 'walls' and air ducts at ground level. (Courtesy of P. Shepherd)

when they come out of the ground are very susceptible to damage and have to be handled gently. A harvester also needs to be able to separate any stones and clods of earth which could cause damage *(Figure 11.15)*; and it needs to be able to deliver the potatoes into a bulk tank or trailer smoothly. They must not be dropped from any height otherwise they will bruise and have to be rejected in the sorting process. Peter Shepherd worked with the machinery manufacturers Johnsons of March to try to develop an appropriate machine but after several trials this was abandoned and Worth Farms started to use the German Grimme harvesters, a modern version of which is still in use today.

Figure 11.14
Permanent Dickie pies at Holbeach.
(Courtesy of P. Shepherd)

Figure 11.15.
Clods at harvest. (GN02068, Gary Naylor)

Figure 11.16
Inspecting potatoes prior to storage using a Herbert Grader. (GN01908, Gary Naylor)

with refrigeration. The rest of the crop was in bulk stores and 'Dickie pies' *(see Chapter 10.1)*.

The area of potatoes grown increased to 400 acres, 100 acres of which were rented from others. More equipment was needed to deal with this increased volume and in 1995 a new Herbert grader was installed indoors which cleaned, sorted, and separated any clods. A manual picking table removed the green or bad potatoes, then the potatoes were sorted by size with the larger ones being cleaned again, but not washed, put in boxes and taken to cold storage *(Figures 11.16 & 11.17)*. There is a rigorous quality control process particularly to detect bruising. More than 5% bruising in a load indicates a need to modify the harvesting or handling techniques.

Figure 11.17
Size grading on the Herbert grader.
(GN01921, Gary Naylor)

By 2005 Worth Farms had expanded to grow 900 acres of potatoes which required two harvesters, ten trailers and a thirty strong labour gang from Eastern Europe. But in 2010 they changed the planting system, reducing the area to 650 acres and using only one planter and one harvester. Only the best land is now used to produce a better quality product which is more cost effective as there is less wastage and the potatoes command higher prices.

The relationship with QV helps to secure the best prices and they insist on quality. 50% of the crop is contracted to QV at a fixed price. The rest is also sold to QV or Manor Fresh but on a variable market price basis.

There were operational changes in 2009; a Production Manager replaced the farm agronomist and farm foreman with external agronomists advising on the latest crop husbandry. The external agronomists have up to the minute knowledge and expertise, advising on fertility, PCN, seeding rates, crop protection and other technical matters, whilst Worth Farms still decide how much of what variety to grow and where to grow it. *Maris Piper (Figure 11.18), Melody, Marfona* and *Cara* are still the main varieties. Whilst the soils around Holbeach are ideal for potatoes, there is one disadvantage and that is that the ground water is saline and so cannot be used for irrigation. The yields therefore are not as high as they could be with irrigation but this is balanced to some extent as there is no cost for water extraction. Worth Farms now produce about 15,000 tonnes per annum using the most up to date equipment *(Figures 11.19 & 11.20)*.

Figure 11.18
Maris Piper variety in flower.
(GN01198, Gary Naylor)

The **Howard** family has been farming at Nocton since 1742 but its involvement with potatoes really started at the beginning of the Second World War when the five acres planted before the war became thirty acres during and after the conflict. **Chris Howard** recalls that prisoners of war did most of the potato picking initially; after the war Irish workers or ex-Land Army women provided the labour. Although based in the same parish, the Howards had no direct involvement in the Smith's potato estate at Nocton, though they did grow some potatoes for them, mainly *Records* which are a high dry-matter potato suitable for making into crisps. In 1963 Chris was one of the founder members of a farmers' co-operative of local growers around Branston which has developed and grown to become the major business now known as Branston Ltd, still based in the village of Branston to the south of Lincoln. Chris Howard has had a continuous involvement with that development. The farmers co-operative started as a buying group, to bulk buy fertiliser and other supplies to minimise costs. The group moved into pea harvesting in a big way as frozen peas started to become popular but in 1967 they turned their attention to potato growing as the potential for that market changed when the use of irrigation for potato crops was introduced. This had the effect of greatly increasing yields thus increasing the profitability. The group was formalised as **Branston Potatoes Ltd** in

Figure 11.19
4 row Miedema potato planting system with AVR G Force rotary cultivator and Team Amistar applicator
(GN02055, Gary Naylor)

Figure 11.20
Grimme 220 Varitron harvester at work.
(GN02062, Gary Naylor)

1968 with seven members initially negotiating contracts with chip and crisp producers. The company is now one of the largest farmer-controlled produce businesses in the UK.

In 1973/4 the group started washing and bagging their own produce and in 1987 a pre-pack plant was added to the site. Chris Howard has maintained his involvement and became Chairman in 1986. His family farm, now run by his son Robert, still supplies potatoes to the company. More growers joined the group to help fund the development and it was at that time that the relationship with the supermarket Tesco began. Since the late 1980s Tesco has grown massively but the relationship with the now named **Branston Ltd.** has remained strong and indeed developed to the point where Branston now supply some two-thirds of all potatoes sold through the largest supermarket chain in the country.

In order to do this Branston has taken over packing plants in other parts of the country and now has premises in Perthshire and Somerset as well as Lincolnshire. They also have contracts with growers all over the country, as well as sourcing from abroad when needed. Branston contract for about 60% of its needs in advance, the other 40% is on a 'free buy' basis, sometimes but not always from the same growers. The price offered depends on a variety of factors including the variety of potato, the month harvested, and the quality. Branston employ about ten agronomists who advise farmers to help to minimise production costs and improve quality *(Figure 21)*. In total there are 264 growers in the Branston Producer Groups, sixty-seven (25%) of whom are based in Lincolnshire. 62,000 tonnes of Lincolnshire-grown potatoes were processed at Branston in 2009, from a total of 161,000 tonnes, so county growers like David Armstrong make a significant contribution to the business. There are also buyers and traders whose job is to ensure that the packing lines at the factory are full every day and that growers are getting a proper return.

Branston concentrates on supplying fresh potatoes, some of which are just washed and packed while others are prepared in different ways as 'convenience food'.

The company delivers about 240,000 metric tonnes of potatoes to Tesco every year; this is some 20% of the total UK market. The type and quantity required are ordered every day. Pre-packs (i.e. the washed potatoes in polythene bags on supermarket shelves) are delivered to nine or ten regional distribution centres and from there are transported to individual stores. All those packed at Branston have BS stamped on, and a batch number and grower reference so that there is complete traceability *(Figure 11.22)*.

Branston has recently built a new anaerobic digestion plant which uses waste potatoes and peelings to generate electricity for the site. The washing water is recycled and energy efficiency is a priority to reduce costs as much as possible. Branston is also at the forefront in terms of presentation and has recently been awarded a top national advertising award by the transport industry

Figure 11.21
Young crop with one root exposed for testing.
(Courtesy of Branston Ltd.)

Figure 11.22
Potatoes packed in polythene bags ready for distribution to Tesco supermarkets.
(Courtesy of Branston Ltd.)

in its 'Livery of the Year' competition. Branston has designed 14 original liveries for their delivery vehicles. The design shown in *Figure 11.23* is based on an idea suggested by a local schoolgirl Chloe Dearden and refers to the popular band 'Take That'. The future for the company looks positive but there is a constant need for innovation and to be responsive to customer demand.

The same is true at QV Foods, the marketing branch of A. H. Worth & Co. Ltd. where there has been a similar story of developing the packing and preparation of the product in response to the requirements of the supermarkets. **Bill Carter** has worked for the company since 1973. Having developed an interest in frozen vegetable products at agricultural college, he initially worked with the frozen peas operation of the Holbeach Marsh Co-operative, which was the backbone of the business at that time, although the Worth family itself always concentrated on the potatoes. Main crop *King Edward* and then *Maris Piper* were the basic varieties sold, mainly in bags through the wholesale market. Peas and potatoes worked well together as the pea season was short, only about six weeks, but the sorting and packing of potatoes occupied staff for the rest of the year.

All of the marketing was done through the Co-operative. The farmers received a monthly income depending on their input, but then there was a 'reckoning up' at the end of the year. The Co-operative was customer driven and needed to ensure a continuity of supply for those customers. But during the 1970s the situation began to change. Supermarkets started buying frozen vegetable products and more people started using them. This began the process which has led to the end of seasonality in the vegetable market and the growth of convenience foods. The Worth family already had links with some supermarkets and were supplying frozen vegetables, particularly to Marks & Spencer (M&S). In 1979 M&S were looking for more convenient fresh potato products that were different and better and asked QV to produce units of four washed, sorted and weighed potatoes for baking, packed and wrapped ready for the shelves. The Potato Marketing Board Research Station at Sutton Bridge *(see Chapter 10)* had developed a similar product, but QV actually weighed each potato to ensure that the four potatoes in the preformed tray were all the same weight. This was the first time in the country that potatoes had been treated in this way. It required significant investment. Computerised weighing equipment was made by GEC; the potatoes had to be carefully selected to ensure evenness of size and complete freedom from defects; they were then washed, dried, weighed and put in a tray with a wrapper and label. Bill Carter was in charge of this project for QV. So the concept of pre-packed selected potatoes was developed in Lincolnshire. These potatoes sold at a premium price which justified the investment.

Figure 11.23
One of the new livery designs for Branston lorries which won the transport industry's top national 'Livery of the Year' award in 2011. It is based on an idea suggested by a local schoolgirl Chloe Dearden and refers to the popular band 'Take That'.
(Steven Hatton, courtesy of Branston Ltd.)

In the 1970s and 1980s the supermarket world was rapidly gaining market share from the wholesalers and it was necessary to understand this world. Holbeach-grown potatoes were good quality and would keep through until May, but supermarkets wanted a twelve month supply and so QV started buying from abroad, and from different parts of UK. They continued to supply M&S, but started business with Sainsbury and Tesco.

The changing nature of the trade meant that the Co-operative was no longer an easy or appropriate marketing organisation, so the Worth family bought out the potato interests of the other farmers and set up a separate marketing company to concentrate just on the potatoes. They developed separate packing lines and buildings for the different supermarkets, dealing with whole potatoes only.

By 2000 the rapid growth of supermarkets began to slow, the wholesale market was greatly reduced, and supermarkets began more competition with rivals for market share. As the supermarket business is consolidating by larger chains taking over smaller ones, so the potato trade is becoming more specialised and concentrated in fewer hands. QV have taken over packing plants in Somerset and Scotland and now pack 3-400,000 tonnes per year, to ensure a continuous supply to the retailers. Some 20% of this quantity is grown in Lincolnshire. M&S potato requirements, marketed under the Manor Fresh brand, are still provided from the Holbeach site but relationships with other supermarkets change from time to time. QV no longer supply Sainsbury or Tesco (this part of the business was sold to Branston) but do supply Asda and other smaller chains.

Demand for convenience products has been growing and QV has responded to this so that the company now peels, chops, dices, adds oil and coatings to produce 'ready to cook' products, but does no actual cooking which is a separate specialised operation and is done by other companies. *(See Chapters 7 & 8).*

All of the above activity takes place to ensure that we, the consumers, can continue to eat potatoes as a significant part of our daily diet in an economical, easy and enjoyable way.

The individuals and organisations named above are not by any means the only Lincolnshire producers involved in the potato trade today. For example, Solanum, the company operating from the premises which used to be part of the Potato Marketing Board Sutton Bridge Research Station, are major suppliers to Waitrose and the Co-operative Society; whilst the erstwhile premises of Boston Potatoes at Kirton are now run by Albert Bartlett, the Scottish potato company; and there are still some 374 individual growers in Lincolnshire. But the examples above do give a cross-section of the industry today, from the small individual growers to the major supermarket suppliers. It all adds up to a significant industry in the county, and a significant source of employment. From the great entrepreneurs of the early twentieth century to the national companies of today, Lincolnshire can lay some claim to being THE potato county.

Acknowledgements

I am greatly indebted to the individuals and companies mentioned in this article for their willing co-operation and interesting stories. Their expertise and enthusiasm is awe-inspiring.

Endnotes

1 Potato Council, *Production and Price Trends 1960-2009*, August 2010 edition

2 Potato Council data for 2009, *e-mail communication from Market Intelligence Department*

3 Potato Council, *Consumption & Processing in GB; Annual Trends June 1988-May 2010 Fig. 1.*

4 Potato Council, *Consumption & Processing in GB; Annual Trends June 1988-May 2010 Fig. 3.*

5 Shepherd, Peter, *A H Worth 50 Years Ago, Chronicle of Peter Shepherd during his 18 months as a farm student,* Viewpoint Supplement, May 2000, Issue 16.

6 Shepherd, *Ibid.*

Chapter 12

SOME RECIPES FOR A VERSATILE FOOD

Compiled by Catherine Wilson and Stewart Squires

'Potatoes, more than any other food product, help to make meat and fish go a long way. …The woman who has to make a penny do the work of a shilling would starve if she couldn't rely on potatoes'.[1] Easily grown in back gardens and on allotments, as well as on a field scale, potatoes became an important part of everyone's diet in the UK by the middle of the nineteenth century and, as the above quotation indicates, were particularly important for the less well-off. Even in the twenty-first century, when there are many alternatives, each person in the UK eats approximately 90 kg per year in a bewildering variety of forms. Potatoes are still one of the cheapest and most nutritious foods available to us.

The potato is the ultimate in flexible food. There are dozens of varieties readily available today and new ones are still being developed. They each have their own characteristics in terms of shape, size, colour, and cooking qualities. They can be eaten small, new and lightly boiled with mint, served with butter; cold as salad potatoes; baked whole in their skins just with butter or with a range of different hot or cold fillings; roasted in the oven as an essential accompaniment to any Sunday or Christmas dinner; or just plain boiled or mashed. They are just as essential as part of that favourite take-away, fish and chips. They are suitable for vegetarians, vegans and those with dairy or gluten allergies. They can also be eaten in a variety of shapes and flavours as crisps and other potato-based snacks. As well as being cooked in standard and obvious ways, potatoes can be used in an endless variety of different recipes – they can even be used to make sherry. The more traditional recipes reflect the fact that potatoes were probably readily available in a rural community and as they were cheap (or 'free' if home grown) they were used imaginatively in place of more expensive ingredients that had to be bought.

Everyone will have their own favourites. Here we offer a small selection of recipes old and new, some of which have been tested by the editors – Stewart Squires did the cooking, Catherine Wilson did the tasting!

The older recipes have been printed in their original form to retain their period flavour. Where information was lacking and to enable their use for the present day additional details are in italics.

Endnote

1 Elizabeth Craig, *Potato Recipes*, Potato Marketing Board, 1936.

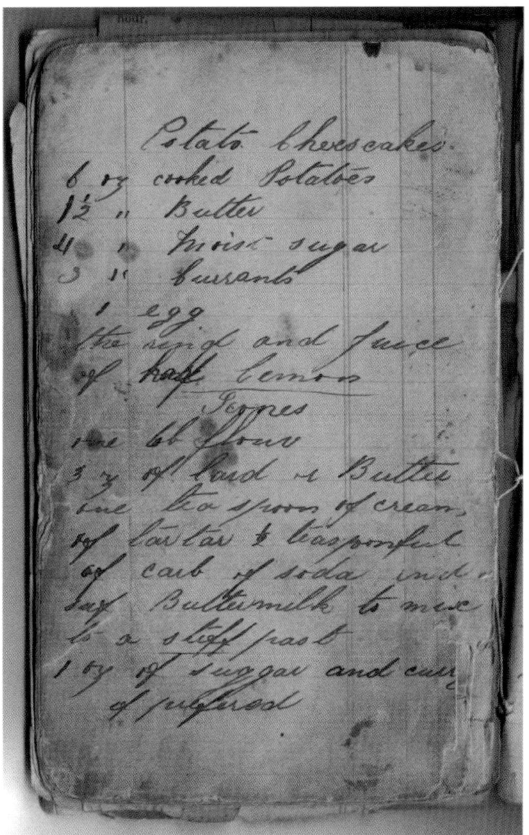

Potato Cheesecakes
6 oz cooked Potatoes
1½ " Butter
4 " moist sugar
3 " Currants
1 egg
the rind and juice
of half lemon

Scones
one lb flour
3 oz of lard or Butter
one tea spoon of cream
of tartar & teaspoonful
of carb of soda and
sour Buttermilk to mix
to a stiff past
1 oz of suggar and curr
of pulferred

Figure 12.1
The handwritten recipe from Rose Hodson's cookery book. This is typical of the time when recipes were handed down from mother, neighbour or friend and, because cooking was by a coal fired range, included no temperatures or cooking times. (Via her great granddaughter, Julie Squires)

From the recipe book of Rose Hodson, Nettleham, c1900

Figure 12.2
Potato Cheesecake.
(Cake and photo by Stewart Squires)

Potato Cheesecake

6oz cooked potatoes
1.5oz butter
4oz moist sugar
2oz currants
1 egg
Rind and Juice of half a lemon.

Cream butter and sugar together, gradually add egg. Add cold mashed potato, currants and the lemon. Line an 8 inch pie plate with shortcrust pastry, put the mixture in, and bake at Gas Mark 4/180C/350F for 35/40 minutes.

From the recipe book of Mrs Kathleen Clark, born at Epworth in December 1899, died at Tickhill in March 1986, via her niece Mrs Fiona Fleming

Potato scones

1lb floury potatoes
2 teaspoon salt
2 oz butter
4 oz Self Raising flour

Mash potatoes; add salt, butter & flour. Make into a stiff mixture, turn on to a floured board, and roll to ½ inch thickness. Cook on greased pan or hot oven about 5 minutes on each side. Makes about 12.

Potato pancakes

Makes 8. Goes well with bacon, eggs, sausage etc.

1½ lb potatoes
1 onion weighing 3 to 4 oz
2 eggs size 2 or 3 lightly beaten
3 level tablespoons of flour
½ level teaspoon baking powder
1 level teaspoon salt
¼ level teaspoon pepper
2 tablespoon of oil or fat for frying

Peel and grate potatoes & onion into bowl and leave 5 minutes then drain excess liquid. Stir in eggs, flour, baking powder, salt and pepper. Divide the mixture into 8 or 9 spoonfuls and drop into fat, flatten with fish slice. Cook 4 minutes on each side until well browned.

Scalloped potatoes

2lb sliced potatoes
1 teaspoon salt, pepper & paprika
2oz plain flour
1oz butter
Milk

Butter a fireproof dish, place a layer of potatoes, sprinkle well with salt and pepper and paprika then sprinkle with a little of the flour and a third of the butter. Repeat until dish is full, then pour in milk in side of dish until it comes up to the last layer. Cover and bake. When done bake uncovered till brown. To vary sprinkle with grated cheese or onion.

Hot potato salad

2 small teaspoon sugar
¼ teaspoon salt
¼ teaspoon dry mustard
¼ teaspoon pepper
¼ cupful vinegar
¼ cupful of water
1 dessert spoon full of bacon dripping or butter
½ tablespoon flour
1 egg yolk or whole egg
1 quart (2 pints) of sliced boiled potatoes
1 minced onion
1 cupful of finely shredded celery or diced cucumber

Mix sugar with salt, mustard and pepper, stir in vinegar and water; pour into saucepan and bring quickly to boil. Rub butter into flour, stir in boiling mixture then stir in the egg. When blended return to pan and boil for 5 minutes stirring all the time; mix the potatoes with onion and celery or cucumber and leave until cold for cold meal or serve hot with sausages or hot meat.

Homemade Sherry

Cut 4 small potatoes into very thin slices and place in a large bowl together with 2 lb sugar, 1 lb large black raisins. Add ¾ pint of boiling water. Mix ½ oz of yeast with ¼ pint of boiling water and when thoroughly dissolved add this to the other ingredients. Add 1 pint of cold water and allow to ferment (this takes about 12 to 15 days) stirring the mixture each day. The sherry should be filtered into bottles through wine filter papers.

Chocolate Potato Cake

6 oz flour
6oz butter
¼ lb cooked potato
2 teaspoonful baking powder
¼ teaspoon salt
6 oz sugar
1 ½ oz Bournville Cocoa
1 teaspoon vanilla essence
2 tablespoonful water

Cream butter and sugar, add sieved mashed potato, mix in flour, salt, water, vanilla essence, baking powder and cocoa. Mix to a stiff paste. Put into a floured and greased ½ lb cake tin. Bake *(at Gas Mark 4/180C/350F)* for 45 minutes.

Figure 12.3
Chocolate Potato Cake.
(Cake and photo by Stewart Squires)

Potato Recipes by Elizabeth Craig, 1936

The Potato Marketing Board had, as well as its regulatory role, a mandate for encouraging the consumption of potatoes through advertising and providing information to consumers. This included publishing recipe booklets. One such, edited by Elizabeth Craig, was first published in 1934 with subsequent editions in 1935 and 1936. It gives basic nutritional advice as well as simple recipes for classic potato dishes. The detailed instructions suggest that it was aimed at novice cooks. A small selection is reproduced here together with the delightful cartoons by Frederick Parker.

Baked Potatoes

If you want potatoes to be crisp and tender, brush skins with melted dripping or oil before baking. Be very careful how you bake potatoes. If baked too long, or if the temperature of the oven is too low, the potatoes will not be floury.

Figure 12.4
Baked Potatoes

TO BAKE: Choose large even-sized potatoes. Scrub, wash, dry, prick with a fork and bake in a baking tin or on a rack in a moderate oven – *Gas Mark 4/180C/*350F – from ¾ to 1 hr according to size. When soft, make a deep cross-cut on the top of each potato and, holding potato in both hands with a cloth, squeeze it gently until the potato comes up through the opening. Season with salt, pepper and paprika, if liked, to taste. Place a pat of butter in the centre of each. Serve in a hot vegetable dish lined with a lace paper doyley, or a folded dinner napkin, which will absorb the steam.

NOTE: -
1. Turn potatoes once or twice while baking
2. Take care that potatoes do not touch each other in the oven
3. Never put potatoes in a closely covered dish, or they will soon become sodden
4. If baked potatoes are wanted in a hurry, boil them in their skins for ¼ of an hour, then drain and dry. Bake in the usual way until soft.

Potato chips

Cut peeled potatoes into slices ¼ inch thick and then cut these slices into ¼ inch strips. If the potatoes are small they may be cut into eighths.

Figure 12.5
Potato Chips

TO PREPARE CHIPS – Wash, peel and cut the potatoes into chips and allow to soak in very cold water for at least half an hour. Heat 2-3½ lbs. of fat in a deep fat fryer until blue smoke rises from it. The pan should be about half to two-thirds full of fat. Use dripping, lard, butter or oil. Dry the chips thoroughly in a cloth. Put into a frying basket. Lower gently into the fat and fry until the potatoes are soft and just beginning to brown at the edges. Lift the basket out of the fat and allow the fat to reheat until it smokes again. Put in the chips again and cook until golden brown. Drain the chips on soft kitchen paper or tissue paper. Dredge with salt and dish on a plate or dish on which is a plain dish paper.

NOTE:-
1. Don't cook too many chips at once or you will chill the fat. If wanted quickly parboil the prepared chips for 3 minutes. Drain and dry before frying.
2. Always have fat in fryer at least 3 inches deep.

Roast potatoes

There are two ways of roasting potatoes. One is to wash and peel them and put them straight into the baking tin with the meat. A better way is to parboil them before roasting.

Figure 12.6
Roast Potatoes

TO ROAST- Choose medium potatoes of equal size. Wash, pare and rinse about 1¼ hours before the roast is ready to dish up. Arrange potatoes in the bottom of the baking tin and baste them with the dripping. Roast until cooked and brown. Turn occasionally. If not using a self-basting roaster, baste them when you baste the meat. I always boil the potatoes, after paring, for 5 or 10 minutes before roasting, and then they only take from 45 to 60 minutes according to size. Serve in a hot vegetable dish lined with a paper doyley, or round the joint.

NOTE –
1. New potatoes should not be parboiled before roasting
2. If not easy to roast potatoes under the joint, pour some of the dripping into a baking tin and roast as suggested.
3. Sprinkle the potatoes with salt after dishing up.
4. Do not cut potatoes in halves before roasting.

Shepherd's Pie

1lb mashed potato
¼ pint hot milk
1lb cold meat
2oz butter
2 peeled chopped onions
1oz flour
½ pint stock or water
2oz cold ham, if liked

Figure 12.7
Shepherd's Pie

Mince meat or meats finely. Melt 1oz Butter in a stew-pan. Add onion and fry till pale brown. Stir in flour and then the stock or water by degrees. Stir till thick. Season to taste. Add the meat or meats. Place in a greased pie dish. Stir the remaining butter and hot milk into the mashed potatoes and beat well. Spread neatly over the meat. Ornament and prick with a fork. Bake in a hot oven, *(Gas Mark 8/230C/450F)* until brown. Enough for four persons.

Recipe from Down To Earth with British Potatoes, published by the Potato Marketing Board about 1980

Duchess Potatoes

2lb mashed potatoes
2 beaten eggs
3oz butter
Salt and pepper to taste

Figure 12.8
Duchess Potatoes

Stir butter into hot potato. Mix well, then stir in one egg at a time. Season to taste with salt and pepper. Place in a forcing bag with star pipe and squeeze out on a greased baking sheet in snails, roses, pyramids or any shape you want. Brush with beaten egg or melted butter. Bake in a quick oven until brown. Use as a garnish or vegetable. Enough for 6 persons.

Figure 12.9.
Down to Earth with British Potatoes, published by the Potato Marketing Board about 1980.
(Charles Parker Collection)

Spicy Potato Crunch

4oz/125g British Potato Peelings, washed and dried
2oz/50g Plain Flour
½ tspn/1x2.5ml spn Salt
5 tblspn/5x15ml spn Cold Water
Choose <u>one</u> of the following flavourings;
2 tspn/2x5ml spn Curry powder
2 tspn/2x5ml spn Worcestershire sauce
½-1 tspn/ ½-1x5ml spn Marmite
1 tspn/1x5ml spn Chilli Powder
Cooking oil for frying
Cooking time: 2 to 3 minutes each batch

Sieve flour and salt into a bowl. Gradually stir in the water to make a batter. Mix in one of the flavourings. Heat some oil in a large frying pan. When it is hot, dip the potato peelings in the batter and fry in the hot fat in batches until they are crisp and brown. Drain on kitchen paper. Sprinkle with salt and serve as a snack or as a garnish for soup. They are best served hot, but can also be eaten cold.

Recipes from Lincolnshire chef Rachel Green, Tastes of Lincolnshire, 2010, via Mary Powell

Rosti Potatoes

Serves 4

2 large baking potatoes, peeled
2 tsp paprika
2 tbsp vegetable oil

For the rosti potatoes, grate the potatoes onto a clean tea towel, sprinkle with salt, and squeeze out any excess liquid. Place in a bowl and add the paprika, and black pepper. Heat the oil in a frying pan. Spoon some of the potato mixture into an oiled metal cooking ring and pack down well. Remove the ring and repeat the process three more times. Cook the rosti for 5 minutes on each side, until well coloured, then transfer to a non stick baking sheet and finish in the oven for 5 - 10 minutes, or until cooked through.

Caramelised Potatoes

Serves 4-6

500g baby new potatoes, unpeeled
3 tbsp groundnut oil
5cm piece root ginger, finely sliced
3 tbsp brown sugar
3 tbsp Chinese rice wine
1½ tbsp light soy sauce
Sea salt and Sichuan pepper

Add the whole new potatoes to a large pan of cold salted water. Bring to the boil, reduce the heat and simmer for about 35 minutes or until tender. Drain and pat on kitchen paper. Cut the potatoes in half if they are not too small and leave to cool slightly. Heat the oil in a hot wok; add the potatoes and stir fry for about 3 minutes or until lightly browned. Add the ginger and stir fry for 30 seconds. Add the sugar, wine and soy sauce and stir fry for about in 1 minute or until slightly caramelised. Sprinkle with Sichuan pepper and salt and serve immediately.

Gratin of New Potatoes and Lincolnshire Poacher Cheese

Butter for greasing
200ml Milk
500ml Double cream
Salt and pepper
1 tsp grated nutmeg
3 cloves of garlic crushed
750g small new potatoes, scraped and cut into 4
75g grated Lincolnshire poacher cheese

Preheat the oven to Gas Mark 5/190C/375F. Butter a small oven proof dish.

Heat the cream and milk in a heavy-bottomed pan with salt and pepper, garlic and grated nutmeg. Bring to the boil then add the diced new potatoes and stir to thoroughly coat them and simmer for 8 minutes. Pour into the ovenproof dish, top with Lincolnshire Poacher and bake in the oven for 30 minutes, until the top is golden and the potatoes are tender.

Lincolnshire Bubble and Squeak Cakes

1kg mashed potatoes allowed to cool
1 small Lincolnshire cabbage shredded
1 tbsp grated Lincolnshire Poacher Cheese
1 tbsp chopped chives
1 tbsp chopped parsley
1 tbsp butter

Boil the shredded cabbage for 2 mins. and refresh in cold water. Mix the potato, cheese, cabbage, chives and parsley together and season. Shape the mixture into patties. Melt the butter, brush the potato cakes with the melted butter and bake at Gas Mark 4/180C/350F for 15-20 mins.

Potato Wedges

500g potatoes, peeled
2 tbsp vegetable or rapeseed oil

Preheat the oven to Gas Mark 7/220°C/425°F. Cut the potatoes into even sized wedges and toss with the rapeseed oil in a large roasting tin. Season with sea salt and black pepper and roast in the preheated oven for 25 – 30 minutes, checking regularly and stirring to ensure that the potatoes do not stick.

Cajun Pea and Potato Salad with Spring Onion dressing

Serves 4-6

600g Charlotte potatoes
4 spring onions, finely chopped
300g frozen peas
3 boiled eggs shelled and cut into quarters
Dressing:
2tbsp mayonnaise
1 tsp wholegrain mustard
1 tsp Dijon mustard
1 tsp white wine vinegar
2 tsp Cajun spice mix
½ tsp paprika
A little olive oil

Cook the potatoes until just tender, about 18 minutes. Drain and cut into bite sized pieces. Cook the peas in slightly salted boiling water for two minutes and mix with the potato. Toss in the spring onions. Season with sea salt and black pepper. Cook the Cajun spice and paprika in a little olive oil in a small saucepan for about 1 minute on a low heat, cool and add to the mayonnaise along with the wholegrain mustard, Dijon mustard and white wine vinegar. Toss through the warm potatoes and peas. Add the eggs, saving three quarters to garnish along with some chopped parsley or chives.

Figure 12.10
'Potato Pete' Wartime advertisement (by permission of the Imperial War Museum, IWM PST 3746)

GLOSSARY

Acre – traditional measurement of land area in the UK (4,840 sq yards, approx 4,050 sq metres)

Agronomy – the science of soil management and crop production

Ambient – the term used for stores that are not temperature controlled

Bins, boxes, crates – the terms are used interchangeably for wooden containers, usually taking one ton/ne of potatoes, which can be moved by mechanical handler and placed in store, or on lorries for transport and can easily be moved around. These containers are a standardised size but usually have the owner's name on so that they can be returned.

Bulk – potatoes stored loose, not in bins

Bulker – the trailers used to carry loose potatoes to packers or processors

Catch crop – a crop grown between two staple crops, in position or time

Certified seed – potatoes which have been grown specifically for production of the following year's crop. These are carefully graded to a specified size and are guaranteed to be disease free

Chats – potatoes too small for human food chain. Also known as pig potatoes

Chitting – the process of encouraging seed potatoes to send out shoots before planting. This takes place in a light frost-free environment, often a glass house.

Clamp – method of storing potatoes outdoors. Also known as **grave** or **pie**

Clods – hard lumps of earth

Cultivar – a variety of a plant produced from a natural species and maintained by cultivation

Dehydration – removing most of the moisture content of the tubers to convert the potatoes into a powder which can be stored for long periods and made into ready to eat mashed potato which is prepared by adding boiling water

Desiccant – a chemical used to kill off potato haulm before harvest. There are three approved for use at the present time: carfentarzone, Diquat and Glufosinate-ammonia.

Dickie pie – method of storing potatoes using bales of straw and ventilation ducts

Dressing – preparing ungraded potatoes for sale by removing over-size, under-size, damaged and diseased tubers. See also Grading.

Early Potatoes – also known as 'new' potatoes, those harvested at a small size before maturity

Fogging – using chemical suppressant to control the growth of sprouts on potatoes in store

Grading – removing small, oversized, damaged or diseased potatoes from the freshly lifted crop to leave only those suitable for human consumption. See also Dressing

Grave – another name for a clamp, so-called from the supposed resemblance to prehistoric long-barrows found on the Lincolnshire Wolds, and elsewhere

Graving – the process of building the 'grave'

Haulm – the green growth of the potato above ground which needs to be killed off before harvesting. The destruction of potato haulm is necessary to reduce late blight, to reduce interference at harvest, to improve skin set and to control tuber size

Headland – a strip of uncultivated land left alongside an arable field to enable machines to turn

Hectare – metric unit of square measure equal to 10,000 sq metres (2.471 acres)

Hoovering out – lifting potatoes out of the ground at harvest, leaving them on the surface for the potato picker to collect

Limestone Brash – broken stone within the soil

Nematicide – chemical treatment used to prevent the growth of nematodes in the soil

New Potatoes – see 'early' potatoes

PCN, Potato Cyst Nematode – a major potato pest commonly called eelworm, these are 1-mm long roundworms which live on the roots of plants of the *Solanaceae* family, such as potatoes and tomatoes. PCN cause growth retardation and are a pest which can remain active in the soil for 8-10 years

Pie – see 'clamp' and 'grave'

Quota – allocation of acreage to be planted by the Potato Marketing Board for planting by individual growers

Small – potatoes too small for storage as part of the main, ware, crop

Sod – a lump of turf and soil, held together by the roots

Soil nematodes – see PCN

Spinner – a machine which lifts the potatoes and 'spins' them to one side by means of metal revolving tines

Stockfeed – out-grade potatoes sold for animal feed

Ton – imperial unit of weight equal to 2,240 lbs (1,016 kg)

Tonne – metric unit of weight equal to 1,000 kg (2,204 lbs)

Volunteers – small potatoes left in the ground after harvest which grow the following season and are not wanted.

Ware Potatoes - term used for main potato crop ready for sale to the public

Windrow - A term normally applied to a row of cut (mown) hay or grain crop which is left to dry before processed further. By analogy, the term may also be applied to a harvested row of any other crop, or indeed the row of stones left by a destoning machine

CONTRIBUTORS

Peter Dewey is Emeritus Reader in Economic History, Royal Holloway, University of London. He has published books on British agriculture in the First World War, the British economy between 1914 and 1945, and the history of the British farm machinery industry since 1800. He was for many years a member of the Executive Committee of the British Agricultural History Society, and served as Secretary to the Society between 1998 and 2002.

Jim Godfrey OBE was brought up on a farm near Caistor; he is a director with his brother and two sons of their farming companies. He is a Council Member of the Biotechnology and Biological Sciences Research Council, a non executive director of the Rural Payments Agency, a member of the Nuffield Scholarship Selection Panel and a director of the Lincolnshire Rural Support Network. He is a former chairman of The Scottish Crop Research Institute, The Potato Marketing Board, Sentry Farming Group plc, the International Potato Centre, and of the Alliance of the 15 Consultative Group on International Agricultural Research Centres which he represented with Governments, the United Nations and the World Bank. He received the OBE for services to agricultural research, the World Potato Congress Industry Award, an Honorary Doctorate from Reading University, and a special British Potato Council Award. He is a Fellow of both the Institute of Directors and the Royal Agricultural Societies.

Abigail Hunt started her career in museums over ten years ago, moving into Further and Higher Education in 2008. She started researching for a PhD at the University of Lincoln in 2003 and is due to complete her thesis in 2011. Her area of academic interest is changing agricultural practice during the twentieth century and its representation in museums in the context of Lincolnshire. She is particularly interested in the changing roles of women in the agricultural sector, mechanisation, land use, and social structures and how associated historical narratives are embodied in museum collections and interpretation.

Dennis Mills learned about potato growing from his farmer grandfather and market gardener father, but his direct experience has been limited to the back garden. He has written widely on rural history, with special reference to the differences between estate villages where large farms predominated and open villages where there were many small farms. He published a major study as *Lord and Peasant in Nineteenth Century Britain*, Croom Helm, 1980. With his wife, Joan, he has recently written *Traditional Farmsteads and Farming at Branston,* to be published by the Branston History Group in 2011.

Charles Parker was born in North Lincolnshire and has spent most of his working life in the County. From 1985 to 1994 he worked as a Field Auditor for the Potato Marketing Board. This entailed visiting growers, potato merchants, processors and other organizations in the fruit and vegetable trade to check plantings and records of sales of potatoes. He was also responsible for checking Area Office contracts with growers during intervention buying programmes and also spent some time at the Sutton Bridge Experimental Station.

Alan Stennett is a Lincolnshire-based writer and broadcaster specialising in farming and agricultural history. The son of a Lincolnshire farmer, he has worked for the BBC since joining the staff in London in 1964. After working for the World Service there and in Cardiff, he was a member of the team which set up BBC Radio Lincolnshire in 1980. He left the staff in 1994 to go freelance, but has continued to produce and present the Lincolnshire Farming programme for the station. Alan was Managing Editor for Independent Farm Business News, which supplied journalism content to the Farming On-line website, and contributes to a number of farming and other publications. He has written five books on Lincolnshire dialects, lost railway lines, the Fens and farming, and has scripted and voiced the commentary for over 50 videos and DVDs with Primetime Videos of Boston. He lives with his wife, Sue, in Woodhall Junction, an old railway station on the banks of the Witham close to Kirkstead Bridge.

Stewart Squires is a long serving member of the Society for Lincolnshire History and Archaeology. For several years Chairman of the Industrial Archaeology team he is currently the Chairman of the Society. A Chartered Town Planner by profession, specializing in historic buildings, he has written extensively about the County's transport and farming history, including *The Lincolnshire Potato Railways,* the second edition published in 2005.

David J. Taylor B.Sc.A.M.A. is the Local History Assistant at North Lincolnshire Museum, where he has worked for many years. He has written four books about the history of the Scunthorpe area, and his interest in crisp making began when he undertook an oral history project about Riley's Potato Crisps and its successor companies in 2004.

Catherine Wilson, OBE is a 'retired' museum professional who retains a lively interest in all aspects of museums both locally and nationally. She moved to Lincolnshire in 1964 and worked for museums in the county until 1983 when she became Director of the Norfolk Museums Service. With no previous experience of, or family background in, agriculture she became fascinated by all aspects of rural life in Lincolnshire whilst working at the Museum of Lincolnshire Life. She is particularly interested in machinery and the processes of agriculture. She is a member of the Rural Museums Network, and has undertaken a number of surveys of agricultural collections in museums for the Network, most recently focussing on ploughs. Her interest in potato growing and marketing stems from a visit to Branston Ltd. some 10 years ago.

Tony Worth has spent most of his working life in Holbeach Marsh in South Lincolnshire. After gaining a degree in Natural Sciences in 1962, he spent some years in Australia as a Farm Management Consultant before returning to the family farm in 1968. Together with his father, he formed and ran Holbeach Marsh Co-operative which graded and marketed potatoes grown by local farmer members to the London Terminal Markets under the QV Brand. It also grew and harvested vining peas for the frozen market. He was Managing Director of the co-operative and of the farming company of A H Worth and Company Limited for many years. The latter company bought out the other farmer members to become QV Foods Limited in 1995.

He has been active in the Lincolnshire Branch of the CLA, the local Drainage Board and the Welland and Nene Local Flood Defence Committee, all of which he has chaired. He also chaired the Lincolnshire Probation Board and was High Sheriff in 1990/91. He was a member of the Project Company for the University in Lincolnshire and a founding member of the Board of Governors of what became the University of Lincoln. He is currently Lord-Lieutenant of Lincolnshire and his eldest son, Duncan, now runs the family business.

INDEX

Page numbers in **bold** refer to illustrations